THE HEALTHY
SPIRALIZER
COOKBOOK

THE HEALTHY
SPIRALIZER
COOKBOOK

*Flavorful & Filling Salads, Soups, Suppers,
and More for Low-Carb Living*

ROCKRIDGE
PRESS

GETTING STARTED WITH ZOODLES
and Other Spiralized Dishes

Hungry for a filling, flavorful, and healthy meal? There's a vegetable for that.

The versatile zucchini: The star of your future zoodle obsession, zucchini make wonderful spaghetti and fettuccine noodles. They really are fantastic dripping with your favorite sauce, as in the classic Spaghetti and Meatballs on page 182 and the tasty and comforting Chicken Zoodle Soup on page 94.

The humble carrot: From pancakes to salads to casseroles, carrots add sweetness, crunch, and lots of vitamin A. Carrots make especially tasty rice. Try them in the Carrot Paella on page 126. They are also yummy in baked sweets, like the Carrot Muffins recipe on page 210.

The better-than-a-potato sweet potato: If you're eating low-carb, chances are you are avoiding potatoes. Sweet potatoes in moderation, however, work well within the framework of a reduced-carbohydrate plan. They are wonderful in savory dishes, such as Sweet Potato Cakes with Orange-Sriracha Aioli on page 116, as well as in sweets, such as in the Avocado-Chocolate Mousse on Spiced Sweet Potato Nests on page 214.

The refreshing cucumber: Cucumbers have such a clean flavor and crisp freshness that work perfectly in salads, such as the Cucumber and Strawberry Salad with Orange Vinaigrette on page 71. They are also delicious in soups and stews. Try the Coconut, Ginger, and Shiitake Soup with Cucumber Noodles on page 84.

CONTENTS

9

Classic Cravings

10

Baked Sweets

11

Kitchen Staples

INTRODUCTION

There are few culinary experiences as satisfying as twirling long strands of pasta around your fork and taking a big, satisfying bite. With your spiralizer you can still enjoy that mouthful—and bowlful—of spaghetti but, if it's zucchini spaghetti, you'll finish the meal feeling good, rather than good and stuffed, too.

Veggie spaghetti, of course, is only the beginning of what your spiralizer can do to help you get flavorful, fun, and low-carb meals on the table. For breakfast, slide your eggs on top of cheesy sweet potato nests flavored with cinnamon and ginger. With lunch, try a confetti of spiralized carrot and apple with shaved fennel. A hearty beef stew with celeriac noodles may become your favorite weekend dinner. Or if animal products aren't a part of your diet, raw pad thai with zucchini noodles might just become your go-to meal in minutes. Your spiralizer will even make it possible for you to turn veggies into rice. No wonder professional chefs are beginning to embrace this kitchen tool right along with home cooks.

Just because you've chosen a healthier lifestyle doesn't mean you have to give up your favorite comfort foods—or, at least, the essence of what makes those foods your favorites. If you're a low-carber or you're on a gluten-free diet, it's likely you miss pasta and rice dishes. But when you think about it, it isn't necessarily the flavor of the pasta or the rice you miss. Rather, it is the delicious things you put on top of them or mix in. And you can still enjoy many of those sauces and savory ingredients. Here you'll find plenty of choices for building tasty meals and snacks, regardless of your dietary preferences—low-carb, Paleo, vegan, vegetarian, or gluten-free.

With your easy-to-use spiralizer (regardless of whether it has two, three, or four blades), a few simple cooking techniques, and the array of recipes you'll find in this cookbook, you can prepare delicious recipes certain to please your palate while helping you maintain a lower-carbohydrate, healthier lifestyle. Start noodlin'!

1

USE YOUR NOODLE

A Spiralizer Starter Guide

Spiralizers, also called spiral vegetable slicers, suddenly seem to be everywhere. For people looking for interesting new ways to add healthy produce to their diet, spiral vegetable and fruit slicers are just the ticket. Using this simple kitchen tool, you can turn a whole vegetable, such as a zucchini or sweet potato, into long, noodle-like spirals that can replace pasta or, with the help of a food processor, rice. Vegetables never looked or tasted better.

Why Spiralize?

You probably already know why you're into spiralizing, but there are so many great health-related reasons. Who wouldn't benefit from a diet that is high in fruits, vegetables, and fiber, and low in processed white foods like pasta and rice? For many, however, cutting carb-heavy foods and adding in fresh, naturally lower-carb foods isn't an option; it's a matter of health or sickness.

In 2012, the journal *Obesity Reviews* published an article that found that low-carb diets were effective for reducing weight and cardiac risk factors. Many people now adopt low-carb diets as a way to lose weight and improve health. However, the biggest challenge of a low-carb diet is staying the course over the long term. The spiralizer makes it possible to eat all kinds of meals that seem incompatible with a low-carb diet by creatively transforming vegetables and fruits. The result: Long-term low-carb living is getting easier every day.

Beyond cutting carbs, increasing your intake of vegetables just makes good sense. According to the USDA, some of the primary health benefits of a vegetable-rich diet include protection against heart attack and stroke, reduced risk of some types of cancer, and better weight control.

Who Should Spiralize?

Of course everyone should spiralize. There's simply no better (and more visually appealing) way to up the veggie content in your meals—not to mention the meals you prepare for your family, too, picky kids included. But although spiralizing is good for everyone, people on one or more of the following diets will especially benefit from using this handy kitchen tool:

Gluten-free (celiac) diets: According to the University of Chicago's Celiac Disease Center, three million Americans are affected by celiac disease, an autoimmune condition that damages the small intestine whenever gluten is ingested. Pasta is made from wheat, which contains gluten. WebMD notes that while there is no cure for celiac disease, the only effective treatment is total elimination of gluten from the diet. While there are gluten-free pastas available, many are high in refined carbohydrates. Spiralized noodles made from vegetables provide a healthy and completely gluten-free option for people with celiac disease and nonceliac gluten sensitivity.

Low-carb and semi-low-carb diets: Pasta and rice contain too many carbs for someone on a low-carb diet. Typically, these diets range from 20 grams to 100 grams per day, depending on how restrictive they are. One cup of pasta contains about 80 grams of carbs, so even a single serving may blow the carb count out of the water for the day. Replacing pasta with spiralized veggies, however, keeps carbs in check.

Paleo diet: This type of diet typically includes fruits and vegetables, nuts and seeds, and animal proteins while eliminating grains, legumes, processed foods, and industrial seed oils. Spiralized vegetables can add variety to ancestral diets, which might otherwise become monotonous.

Low-calorie diets: Spiralized vegetables will help anyone who is trying to lose weight by consuming fewer calories. Veggie noodles have far fewer calories than their pasta counterparts.

Vegan and vegetarian diets: For those on a plant-based diet, spiralized vegetables provide a new and interesting way to eat plant foods.

What to Spiralize

While spiralizing is for everyone, it isn't necessarily for every fruit or vegetable. Some simply don't have enough structure, and they will turn to mush. If you don't want to wind up with a shapeless pile of wet fruit or veggies, then it's best to stick to produce with the following qualities:

Firm flesh: Fruits or vegetables that spiralize well have reasonably firm flesh: Think zucchini, jicama, beets, and radishes. Vegetables with slightly softer flesh, like eggplant, will spiralize, but with difficulty.

No core: If a fruit or vegetable has a core, then it probably won't spiralize. But some produce, such as apples, can be spiralized whole because the small seeds just pop out, and cabbage can be spiralized by cutting off the end with the core.

Solid inside: The fruit or vegetable must be solid all the way through, like a carrot or beet.

At least an inch and a half in diameter: Anything thinner won't spiralize well, even if you're using an hourglass spiralizer.

Two inches long or longer: Since the spirals come from the length of the fruit or vegetables, if you have a very short piece of produce, you'll also have very short spirals. What fun is that?

SOME THINGS CAN'T BE SPIRALIZED

Once you discover just how much fun it is to spiralize fruits and vegetables, you just might get spiralizer fever and try to spiralize everything. Some fruits and vegetables aren't great candidates, however. While you're certainly free to experiment, try to avoid fruits and vegetables that have:

- High water content, such as a melon
- Very soft flesh, like a banana or avocado
- Large pits, like a peach
- Hollow cores, like a cantaloupe or coconut
- Extremely hard cores, like a pineapple
- Seeds scattered throughout, like a watermelon

Choosing Produce for Low-Carb Eating

If you're a low-carber, you already know that some fruit and vegetables add significantly more to your carb count than others. But your fruit and veggie choices may be influenced by a number of factors, in addition to the number of carbs. For example, if you're in the induction phase of the Atkins diet, which allows a maximum of 20 grams of carbs per day, you probably won't choose a sweet potato, but a zucchini will work just fine. On the other hand, if you're on a semi-low-carb plan, such as the Paleo diet, then you

Will It Noodle?

To noodle or not to noodle? That is the question. Many fruits and vegetables lend themselves very well to spiralizing, while others are just a waste of time. Some fruits and veggies are ready to go into the spiralizer as is (after washing them), while others may take a little bit more prep work, such as peeling, cutting in half, and removing seeds, cores, or pits.

Use this handy chart to help you determine which are super easy, which take a bit more work, and which are best avoided altogether.

IDEAL & EASY		WORTH IT WITH SOME MUSCLE	
Apple	Cut ends flat, remove stem	Broccoli stem	Cut the ends of the stem flat
Beet	Peel, cut ends flat	Butternut squash	Remove the thick round end and the stem, peel
Carrot	Peel, cut ends flat	Cabbage	Cut in half, core, remove outer leaves
Cucumber	Peel, cut ends flat	Celeriac	Remove greens, cut ends flat, peel
Daikon radish	Peel, cut ends flat	Jicama	Cut ends flat, peel
Pear	Peeling is optional, cut ends flat	**SKIP IT**	
Potato, white or russet	Peeling is optional, cut ends flat	Bell pepper	
Rutabaga	Peel, cut ends flat	Eggplant	
Summer squash	Cut ends flat	Leek	
Sweet potato	Peel, cut ends flat	Melon	
Turnip	Peel, cut ends flat	Pineapple	
Zucchini	Cut ends flat		

can choose from a much broader array of fruits and vegetables and still not blow up your carb count. Other factors that reduced-carb diet plans take into account when suggesting a carb count for you are your age, sex, activity level, how well you tolerate carbohydrates, and any relevant medical conditions, such as hypothyroidism and diabetes.

The fruits and vegetables you choose to spiralize will depend on all of the above factors. However, it is important to note that spiralized fruits and vegetables will always be lower in carbohydrates than their processed pasta counterparts.

You may already know that one of the basic mechanisms behind the success of a low-carb diet is blood glucose control, and fiber doesn't raise blood sugar. Yet it is calculated into the total carb count in recipes. That's why many people on reduced-carbohydrate diets subtract grams of fiber from total grams of carbohydrates to calculate what's known as "net carbs." For example, a dish with 15 grams of carbohydrates and 5 grams of fiber calculates as having 10 net grams of carbs. In the recipes in this book, we provide total carbs and fiber information per serving so that you can easily determine the net carb count.

Choosing Organic

When cooking with spiralized produce, you want to find the freshest, healthiest veggies and fruits you can. Choosing organic foods can help you minimize the chemicals you put into your body and lower your overall toxic load. The Environmental Working Group lists the Dirty Dozen vegetables and fruits, which are very high in pesticides. They suggest always buying these fruits and vegetables organic in order to minimize the chemicals you ingest. (See page 233 for the full list.)

There are only a few fruits and veggies on the list that you will spiralize and should always try to buy organic:

- Apples
- Cucumbers
- Potatoes

For your reference, here is a chart of total carb counts for the produce you'll be spiralizing.

FRUIT AND VEGETABLE CARB COUNTS

FRUITS AND VEGETABLES	TOTAL CARBS (PER FRUIT OR VEGETABLE)
Apple (3 inches diameter)	25 grams
Beet (2 inches diameter)	8 grams
Broccoli (1 cup)	6 grams
Butternut squash (¼ medium squash)	30 grams
Cabbage (½ medium)	21 grams
Carrot (7 to 8 inches long)	7 grams
Celeriac (4 inches diameter)	14 grams
Cucumber (8 inches long)	11 grams
Daikon radish (7 inches long)	14 grams
Jicama (½ medium)	29 grams
Pear (3 inches diameter)	27 grams
Russet potato (3 to 4 inches diameter)	67 grams
Summer squash (7 to 8 inches long)	6 grams
Sweet potato (5 inches long)	28 grams
White potato (3 to 4 inches diameter)	58 grams
Zucchini (7 to 8 inches long)	6 grams

You'll notice that the chart above lists russet and white potatoes. While these aren't part of a low-carbohydrate lifestyle, they are great for people who wish to make the most of their spiralizer and don't have any limitations on carbs. You won't find white or russet potato recipes in most of the chapters of this cookbook, with the exception of the Classic Cravings chapter. If you're on a low-carb diet, feel free to replace the white potato or russet with a lower-carb spiralized vegetable. Or just make these recipes occasionally, for a treat.

Other fruits and veggies that are somewhat higher in carbs can still be part of a healthy low-carbohydrate diet, provided you fill the rest of your day with appropriate low-carb choices in order to meet your carb counts. They include apples, pears, jicama, butternut squash, and sweet potatoes, which are all used in this cookbook.

If you still aren't convinced that using a spiralizer will save carbs, check out the differences in carbs between these classic recipes and their spiralized counterparts.

TRADITIONAL DISH	TOTAL CARBS	SPIRALIZED DISH	TOTAL CARBS
Macaroni and cheese	52 grams	Carrot Mac and Cheese (page 199)	12 grams
Pesto with spaghetti	29 grams	Spaghetti with Classic Pesto Sauce (page 192)	12 grams
Shrimp fried rice	42 grams	Daikon Radish Shrimp Fried Rice (page 200)	14 grams
Beef stroganoff with egg noodles	35 grams	Beef Stroganoff with Summer Squash Noodles (page 144)	27 grams
Paella	39 grams	Carrot Paella (page 126)	14 grams

Which Spiralizer Is Best?

With the growing popularity of spiralizers, there are many different brands and types to choose from. They range in price from around $10 to more than $50, and they all have different features. Before you choose your spiralizer, consider how often you think you will use it, how much you want to spend, how important it is to you to make different types of noodles, and how much storage space you can give it.

These spiralizers take up a bit of storage space, but they tend to be very easy to use. Many come with interchangeable blades, allowing you to transform your produce into pasta strands in at least three different widths:

- Spaghetti
- Fettuccine
- Wide-ribboned noodles

Others may have additional blades that allow you to cut angel hair noodles and other shapes, as well.

Popular Brands

There are several popular and well-rated brands of the hand-crank spiralizers, including the following:

- **Paderno spiralizers** come in three- and four-blade versions. Each model has convenient suction cups to hold it in place on the counter.
- **Inspiralizer** has four cutting blades and uses clamps to stay in place on the countertop. There is also a suction base.
- **GEFU Spirafix** is a top-crank, handheld spiralizer. It has two blades that can cut four different widths of noodles.

How It Works

These spiralizers are fairly straightforward, with a blade and a pusher or crank. You attach the vegetable (with the ends trimmed flat) to the pronged holder and push it until it is even with the blade. Then you turn the crank. The spiralizer rotates the vegetable or fruit through the blade, cutting it into the desired shape. The interchangeable blades store and switch easily with a simple snap-in mechanism.

Pros and Cons

Pros: These spiralizers are easy to use and to secure to your countertop (except for the handheld model). They also make the best-looking spiral pasta, giving you long, twisty noodles that are beautiful to behold. The interchangeable blades give you more zoodle choices.

Cons: These spiralizers take up some counter and storage space, and they tend to be more expensive than their hourglass counterparts. If the suction cups don't hold the tool securely, the spiralizer will slide around on your counter, making it difficult to get the job done. In addition, it may take some elbow-grease to attach the fruit or vegetable to the pronged holder.

Ideal Vegetables for Use

These spiralizers will handle pretty much any suitable fruit or veggie like a champ. However, some produce is ideally suited for hand-crank spiralizers, such as beets, zucchini, sweet potatoes, summer squash, and russet or white potatoes.

Get to Know These Veggies

The recipes in this book contain a few uncommon vegetables that you may not have eaten before. Here's what you need to know about them:

Daikon radish looks like a long, fat, white carrot. It is, as the name implies, a member of the radish family. As such, it has a mild, peppery taste, but it doesn't overwhelm a dish. The vegetable is starchy and serves as a great stand-in for potatoes.

Celeriac, also known as celery root, is not the most attractive vegetable around. It has a bumpy, almost dirty looking exterior, which you need to peel with a paring knife before you get to the actual root. The root is white in color, and it has a mild, nutty flavor. It works well in low-carb recipes as a substitute for potatoes or rice.

Jicama is a large, starchy bulb. When eaten raw, it is crispy and refreshing, with a wonderful crunch. It is slightly sweet with a mild flavor. You need to peel the brown skin off the jicama before using it in your spiralizer.

These spiralizers are handheld and small. They typically allow you to cut your veggies into thin spaghetti-like or thick fettuccine-like shapes. Most of them come with a pronged vegetable holder/pusher, as well as a brush for cleaning.

Popular Brands

Many manufacturers make the hourglass models of spiralizers, including:

- Vegetti
- Kitchen Supreme
- Zoodle Slicer
- Brieftons

How It Works

These spiralizers work like a pencil sharpener. You attach the vegetable to the holder/pusher and then put them in the appropriate end of the spiralizer. Twist the vegetable, and as you do, spiraled ribbons come out the other end.

Pros and Cons

Pros: These spiralizers are super easy to use, and they hardly take up any space at all. Because they come with a cleaning brush, they tend to be fairly easy to clean, as well. They are also quite affordable, usually under $30.

Cons: Many people, including the editors at *Cooks Illustrated* magazine, complain that this type of spiralizer tends to produce broken shreds of vegetables, rather than noodles. Because the opening is small, you can use only fairly thin vegetables in this type of spiralizer, and you have to be careful not to get too close to the blade. You'll also be doing a lot of work to get the entire vegetable through the spiralizer. It can be slow going.

Ideal Vegetables for Use

These spiralizers work best with thin vegetables, such as carrots, cucumbers, and zucchini.

Oodles of Noodles

Depending on the spiralizer you choose, you can get anywhere from one to five different types of noodles. In hand-crank models, this requires a simple blade change.

Angel hair noodles are long and very thin. Making these noodles is not possible with every spiralizer, but it is with the recent Paderno four-blade, hand-crank model. Their new blade is called the "angel hair" blade.

Spaghetti noodles are slightly thicker than angel hair. Virtually every spiralizer makes this type of noodle. Use the shredder blade on the Paderno model and the thin-cutting blade on hourglass models. On the Inspiralizer, use blade D.

Linguine noodles are flat, narrow ribbons. To date, they can be made only with the Inspiralizer model using blade C.

Fettuccine noodles are slightly thicker and wider than linguine. Most spiralizers have blades to make these noodles. Use the chipper blade on the Paderno models and blade B on the Inspiralizer. On hourglass models, use the thick-cutting blade.

Ribboned noodles are extra wide, flat, and wavy, like pappardelle pasta. Use the straight blade on the Paderno models and blade A on the Inspiralizer to make ribboned noodles. You cannot make ribboned noodles with the hourglass models.

10 Tips for Spiralizer Success

Using a spiralizer isn't difficult, but there are several things you can do to ensure your success every time you use one.

1. If the spiralizer's suction cups will not stick to the counter, try wetting your finger and rubbing the bottom of the suction cups. Then try sticking them to the counter again.

2. Use hand-crank spiralizers on a smooth surface for best results.

3. Put a plate or bowl under the blade to catch the noodles as they come off the spiralizer.

4. In some cases, the spiralizer makes very long noodles. Use kitchen shears or a knife to snip them into manageable lengths.

5. Choose firm fruits and vegetables. If they have gone soft, then they will not spiralize well.

6. Choose vegetables that fit well on the pusher/holder. The best vegetables are those that are just slightly thicker or slightly thinner than the holder. If vegetables are much too thick, cut them in half lengthwise.

7. If the fruit or vegetable you are using has a curve to it, cut it in half at the curve so it goes through the spiralizer more efficiently.

8. When using a hand-crank spiralizer, be sure to cut the ends of the fruit or vegetable flat so they will stick on the holder.

9. Vegetables and fruit tend to have a lot of water in them. Pat them dry with a paper towel after spiralizing, or leave them in a colander over the sink for about 30 minutes. Then pat them dry.

10. Cook noodles and sauce separately, rather than cooking the noodles in the sauce. This will keep your sauce from getting watery.

Making the Recipes in This Book

No matter which spiralizer you own, you should be able to make all of the recipes in this book—or slightly adapted versions of them. That's why every recipe in chapters 2 through 10 will include one or two spiralizer icons that look like this:

When you see the hand-crank icon, you know that you can use your hand-crank spiralizer to make the recipe. Below the icon, the specific blade to use with the Paderno or Inspiralizer models is noted.

When you see the hourglass icon, you know that you can use this type of spiralizer to make the recipe. Below the icon, the specific blade to use is noted (thin-cutting or thick-cutting). If you do not see the hourglass icon, that means the recipe calls for a fruit or vegetable that is not easy to spiralize with this type of spiralizer. In these cases, a tip will be provided to let you know how to adapt the recipe for your hourglass-shaped spiralizer.

In chapter 11, you won't find any recipes that call for a spiralizer. Instead, these will be recipes for the must-have stocks, condiments, and sauces that you want to have on hand for flavoring your noodles.

A Flavor for All Diets

Just because you're on a special diet doesn't mean you need to give up your favorite foods. While some ingredients may not work with your diet, there are alternatives that will still give you the same flavor profile and textural properties while meeting your dietary requirements.

INGREDIENT	GLUTEN-FREE ALTERNATIVE	PALEO-FRIENDLY ALTERNATIVE	VEGAN ALTERNATIVE
Soy Sauce	Wheat-free tamari or coconut aminos	Coconut aminos	N/A
Cheese	N/A	Grass-fed raw cheese Cashew cheese	Cashew cheese Soy cheese Nutritional yeast
Flour	Gluten-free all-purpose flour Tapioca flour	Tapioca flour Almond meal flour Coconut flour	N/A
Cornstarch	N/A	Arrowroot powder	N/A
Butter	N/A	Grass-fed butter Coconut oil	Vegan butter Coconut oil
Milk	N/A	Coconut milk Almond milk	Rice milk Almond milk Coconut milk
Eggs	N/A	N/A	Ground flaxseeds and water
Sugar	N/A	Stevia Raw honey Pure maple syrup	N/A

2

BREAKFASTS

SWEET POTATO AND PEAR BREAKFAST RISOTTO

PREP TIME: 10 MINUTES / COOK TIME: 20 MINUTES

IDEAL FOR HAND-CRANK SPIRALIZERS
- Shredder blade
- Blade D

SERVES 4

GLUTEN-FREE,
PALEO-FRIENDLY, VEGAN

PER SERVING: Calories: 175;
Total Fat: 14g; Saturated Fat: 12g;
Cholesterol: 0mg; Total Carbs: 13g;
Fiber: 3g; Protein: 1g

Spiralizer alternative: *If you have an hourglass spiralizer, cut the potato in half lengthwise before using it or substitute a carrot. Spiralize using the thin-cutting blade.*

Risotto for breakfast? Sure! When it's made with sweet potatoes, pears, and coconut milk, it's the perfect way to start your morning. Think of it as a creamy, slightly sweet hot breakfast cereal, minus the grains but with tons of flavor.

1 sweet potato, peeled, ends cut flat,
    and spiralized into spaghetti noodles
2 tablespoons coconut oil
1 pear, peeled, cored, and cut into ¼-inch dice
½ cup coconut milk
½ teaspoon ground cinnamon
¼ teaspoon ground nutmeg
Pinch sea salt

1. In a food processor, pulse the sweet potato noodles until it resembles rice, about 20 one-second pulses.

2. In a large sauté pan, heat the coconut oil over medium-high heat until it shimmers.

3. Add the pear and cook, stirring occasionally, until it begins to brown, about 5 minutes.

4. Add the sweet potato rice and cook, stirring occasionally, until it is soft and starts to brown, about 5 minutes more.

5. Stir in the coconut milk, cinnamon, nutmeg, and salt. Cook, stirring frequently, until warmed through, 3 or 4 minutes more.

6. Serve immediately.

CARROT AND WALNUT PANCAKES

PREP TIME: 10 MINUTES / COOK TIME: 10 MINUTES

HAND-CRANK
- Shredder blade
- Blade D

HOURGLASS
- Thin-cutting blade

SERVES 4

GLUTEN-FREE,
PALEO-FRIENDLY, VEGAN

PER SERVING: Calories: 268;
Total Fat: 25g; Saturated Fat: 16g;
Cholesterol: 0mg; Total Carbs: 11g;
Fiber: 3g; Protein: 5g

Sweet, earthy carrots make a great addition to these low-carb pancakes. When making pancake batter, avoid overmixing it; a few little lumps are fine.

2 carrots, peeled, ends cut flat, and spiralized into
    spaghetti noodles
¾ cup almond flour
¼ cup arrowroot powder
¼ teaspoon stevia
1½ teaspoons baking powder
Pinch sea salt
¼ teaspoon ground ginger
½ teaspoon ground cinnamon
1 cup coconut milk
2 tablespoons coconut oil, melted, divided
1 teaspoon vanilla extract
¼ cup finely chopped walnuts

1. Cut the carrot noodles into ½-inch-long pieces. Set aside.

2. In a medium bowl, whisk in the almond flour, arrowroot powder, stevia, baking powder, salt, ginger, and cinnamon.

3. In a small bowl, whisk together the coconut milk, first tablespoon of coconut oil, and vanilla extract.

4. Pour the wet ingredients into the dry ingredients and mix until just combined. Fold in the walnuts and carrots.

5. Heat a nonstick skillet over medium-high heat and brush it with the remaining coconut oil.

6. Pour ¼ cup of batter into the skillet for each pancake. Cook until browned, 3 to 5 minutes. Turn the pancakes and cook for another 3 to 5 minutes. Serve cooked pancakes hot.

GERMAN APPLE PANCAKE

PREP TIME: 10 MINUTES / COOK TIME: 20 MINUTES

 IDEAL FOR HAND-CRANK
SPIRALIZERS
- Straight blade
- Blade A

SERVES 4

GLUTEN-FREE,
PALEO-FRIENDLY,
VEGETARIAN

PER SERVING: Calories: 340;
Total Fat: 32g; Saturated Fat: 26g;
Cholesterol: 123mg;
Total Carbs: 12g; Fiber: 4g;
Protein: 6g

Spiralizer alternative: *An hourglass spiralizer will not work for
this recipe. Instead, peel and
thinly slice the apple.*

*The German apple pancake is a breakfast staple. This large,
puffy pancake tastes best with a sweet-tart apple, such as a
Honeycrisp or Granny Smith. You don't have to peel or core
the apple. Just remove the stem, trim it flat if it won't fit on the
pusher, and it's ready to go.*

1 apple, stemmed, cored, ends cut flat,
    and spiralized into ribbon noodles
¼ cup plus 2 tablespoons coconut oil,
    melted and divided
2 teaspoons ground cinnamon
¼ teaspoon ground nutmeg
½ cup coconut milk
3 eggs
¼ teaspoon stevia
1 teaspoon vanilla extract
2 tablespoons coconut flour
¼ teaspoon baking soda
Pinch salt

1. Preheat the oven to 425°F.

2. Cut the apple ribbons crosswise to make apple slices.

3. In a small ovenproof skillet or sauté pan, heat ¼ cup of
the coconut oil over medium-high heat until it shimmers.
Sprinkle the oil with the cinnamon and nutmeg, and then
place the apple slices in an even layer on the bottom of the
pan. Cook, without stirring, until the apples brown on the
bottom, about 5 minutes.

4. While the apples cook, combine the remaining 2 tablespoons of coconut oil, the coconut milk, eggs, stevia, vanilla extract, coconut flour, baking soda, and salt in a blender. Blend on high speed until well mixed.

5. Pour the batter over the apples. Remove the pan from the heat and transfer it to the oven. Bake until the pancake sets and puffs, 10 to 15 minutes.

6. Cut into slices and serve hot.

BUTTERNUT SQUASH WAFFLES

PREP TIME: 10 MINUTES / COOK TIME: 10 MINUTES

IDEAL FOR HAND-CRANK
SPIRALIZERS

- Shredder blade
- Blade D

SERVES 4

GLUTEN-FREE, PALEO-
FRIENDLY, VEGAN

PER SERVING: Calories: 290;
Total Fat: 28g; Saturated Fat: 22g;
Cholesterol: 0mg; Total Carbs: 13g;
Fiber: 3g; Protein: 4g

Spiralizer alternative: *If you
have an hourglass spiralizer,
replace the butternut squash
with zucchini. Spiralize using
the thin-cutting blade.*

*Butternut squash becomes a delicious low-carb breakfast food
when you cut the spirals into short lengths and combine them
with other low-carb staples, like almond flour and stevia. If you
prefer a less sweet waffle, you can leave out the stevia altogether.*

¼ medium butternut squash, peeled, ends cut
 flat, and spiralized into spaghetti noodles
¾ cup almond flour
½ cup arrowroot powder
2 teaspoons baking powder
1 teaspoon ground cinnamon
½ teaspoon stevia
Pinch salt
2 tablespoons coconut oil, melted and divided
1¼ cups coconut milk

1. Preheat a waffle iron.

2. Cut the squash noodles crosswise into ½-inch-long
pieces and set aside.

3. In a medium bowl, whisk together the almond flour,
arrowroot powder, baking powder, cinnamon, stevia, and salt.

4. In a small bowl, mix 1 tablespoon of the coconut oil
and milk.

5. Pour the wet ingredients into the dry ingredients and
mix until just combined.

6. Fold in the butternut squash noodles.

7. Grease the waffle iron with the remaining 1 tablespoon of the coconut oil.

8. Pour ¼ cup of the batter onto the waffle iron and close it. Cook until browned, about 5 minutes. Repeat until you've used up the batter, greasing the waffle iron with more coconut oil if needed.

9. Serve immediately.

SOUTHWESTERN SWEET POTATO HASH BROWNS
WITH PICO DE GALLO AND AVOCADO

PREP TIME: 15 MINUTES / COOK TIME: 15 MINUTES

 IDEAL FOR HAND-CRANK SPIRALIZERS

- Shredder blade
- Blade D

SERVES 2

GLUTEN-FREE,
PALEO-FRIENDLY, VEGAN

PER SERVING: Calories: 443;
Total Fat: 38g; Saturated Fat: 6g;
Cholesterol: 0mg; Total Carbs: 25g;
Fiber: 8g; Protein: 4g

Spiralizer alternative: *If you
have an hourglass spiralizer,
replace the sweet potato with
4 large, peeled carrots. Spiralize using the thin-cutting blade.*

*The ancho chile and spices give these sweet potato hash browns
a classic Southwestern flavor. The pico de gallo adds more heat,
while the avocado cools it all down. The result is a delicious and
healthy breakfast. Make your own or you can buy pico de gallo
in the refrigerated produce section at your local grocery store.*

FOR THE PICO DE GALLO (MAKES ½ CUP)

½ medium tomato, minced

½ red onion, minced

1 jalapeño pepper, seeded and minced

2 tablespoons chopped fresh cilantro

Juice of ½ lime

¼ teaspoon salt

FOR THE HASH BROWNS

1 sweet potato, peeled, ends cut flat,
    and spiralized into spaghetti noodles

4 scallions (white and green parts), thinly sliced

1 ancho chile, seeded and thinly sliced

4 tablespoons olive oil, divided

1 teaspoon chili powder

½ teaspoon ground cumin

½ teaspoon sea salt

¼ teaspoon freshly ground black pepper

½ avocado, sliced

Mix all the ingredients together in a bowl.

TO MAKE THE HASH BROWNS

1. Cut the sweet potato spirals crosswise into ½-inch pieces.

2. In a large bowl, toss together the sweet potato, scallions, ancho chile, 2 tablespoons of the olive oil, the chili powder, cumin, salt, and pepper.

3. In a large sauté pan, heat the remaining 2 tablespoons of olive oil over medium-high heat until it shimmers.

4. Spread out the sweet potato mixture on the bottom of the pan and cook, without stirring, until it browns on the bottom, about 5 minutes. Flip and cook until browned on the other side, 4 to 5 minutes more.

5. Serve topped with the avocado and pico de gallo.

ZUCCHINI CAKES
WITH PAN-ROASTED MUSHROOMS

PREP TIME: 30 MINUTES / COOK TIME: 20 MINUTES

HAND-CRANK
- Shredder blade
- Blade D

HOURGLASS
- Thin-cutting blade

SERVES 4

GLUTEN-FREE,
PALEO-FRIENDLY, VEGAN

PER SERVING: Calories: 217;
Total Fat: 19g; Saturated Fat: 2g;
Cholesterol: 0mg; Total Carbs: 10g;
Fiber: 4g; Protein: 7g

Zucchini cakes make a tasty breakfast when you top them with savory, meaty mushrooms. You can also use the zucchini cakes as a base for a delicious low-carb open breakfast sandwich. Just use them as you would the bottom of a toasted English muffin. Top them with your favorite breakfast meat, eggs prepared any way you like, and a little bit of cheese.

1 zucchini, ends cut flat and spiralized into
   spaghetti noodles

1 tablespoon plus 1 teaspoon sea salt, divided

1 pound button mushrooms, halved

4 tablespoons olive oil, divided

1 teaspoon chopped fresh thyme

3 garlic cloves, minced and divided

½ teaspoon freshly ground black pepper, divided

½ red bell pepper, finely chopped

3 scallions (white and green parts), finely chopped

1 tablespoon Dijon mustard

Pinch crushed red pepper flakes

¼ cup almond meal flour

1 tablespoon flaxseed meal

3 tablespoons water

1. Preheat the oven to 400°F.

2. In a colander set over the sink, sprinkle the zucchini noodles with 1 tablespoon of the salt and let it sit for 30 minutes to draw out water.

3. Meanwhile, in a large bowl, toss together the mushrooms, 2 tablespoons of the oil, the thyme, 2 minced garlic cloves, ½ teaspoon of the salt, and ¼ teaspoon of the black pepper.

4. Spread out the mushrooms in a large roasting pan and roast until they are browned, about 20 minutes. Remove from the oven and cover with aluminum foil to keep warm while you make the zucchini cakes.

5. Quickly rinse the zucchini to remove the salt and pat it dry with paper towels. Cut the zucchini crosswise into ½-inch pieces.

6. In a large bowl, combine the zucchini, red bell pepper, scallions, the remaining minced garlic clove, mustard, red pepper flakes, almond meal, the remaining ½ teaspoon of salt, and the remaining ¼ teaspoon of black pepper.

7. In a small bowl, whisk together the flaxseed meal and water. Pour into the zucchini mixture and mix well.

8. Form the mixture into 8 cakes.

9. In a large nonstick skillet over medium-high heat, heat the remaining 2 tablespoons of olive oil until it shimmers.

10. Add the zucchini cakes and cook, without moving them, until they brown on one side, 5 to 6 minutes. Flip the cakes and continue to cook until the second side is browned, another 5 to 6 minutes. Blot on paper towels.

11. Serve the cakes topped with the mushrooms.

CARROT, ONION, AND PANCETTA FRITTATA

PREP TIME: 10 MINUTES / COOK TIME: 30 MINUTES

HAND-CRANK
- Shredder blade
- Blade D

HOURGLASS
- Thin-cutting blade

SERVES 4

GLUTEN-FREE,
PALEO-FRIENDLY

PER SERVING: Calories: 386;
Total Fat: 31g; Saturated Fat: 11g;
Cholesterol: 359mg;
Total Carbs: 5g; Fiber: 1g;
Protein: 22g

Caramelizing onions adds a savory sweetness to this frittata, which goes beautifully with the earthy carrots. Leaving the carrots in long, spaghetti-like strands mimics the texture of a pasta frittata without the high amount of carbs.

2 tablespoons olive oil, plus more as needed

4 ounces pancetta, diced

½ onion, thinly sliced

1 carrot, peeled, ends cut flat, and spiralized into spaghetti noodles

8 eggs

¼ cup almond milk

½ teaspoon sea salt

¼ teaspoon freshly ground black pepper

Pinch ground nutmeg

1. In an ovenproof sauté pan, heat the olive oil over medium-high heat.

2. Add the pancetta and cook, stirring frequently, until it is crispy and has rendered its fat. Remove the pancetta with a slotted spoon, leaving the fat in the pan, and set aside on paper towels.

3. Reduce the heat to medium-low. Add the onion to the fat and cook, stirring occasionally, until soft and caramelized, about 20 minutes. Remove the onion with a slotted spoon and set aside.

4. Raise the heat to medium-high. Add the carrot noodles to the remaining fat, adding a bit more olive oil if necessary, and cook, without stirring, until it begins to brown, about 4 minutes. Flip the carrot noodles and cook for another 4 minutes.

5. Preheat the broiler.

6. In a large bowl, whisk together the eggs, almond milk, salt, pepper, and nutmeg until well combined. Fold in the pancetta and onion.

7. Carefully pour the egg mixture over the carrot noodles. Cook on the stovetop until the eggs begin to set, 3 to 4 minutes.

8. Put the pan under the broiler and cook until the frittata is set, golden brown, and puffy, 3 to 5 minutes.

9. Serve immediately.

Ingredient tip: *If you like cheese with your eggs, sprinkle ¼ cup of grated Gruyère cheese over the eggs just before putting them under the broiler.*

ZUCCHINI, MUSHROOM, AND SWISS FRITTATA

PREP TIME: 10 MINUTES / COOK TIME: 15 MINUTES

 HAND-CRANK
- Shredder blade
- Blade D

HOURGLASS
- Thin-cutting blade

SERVES 4

GLUTEN-FREE, VEGETARIAN

PER SERVING: Calories: 274;
Total Fat: 22g; Saturated Fat: 11g;
Cholesterol: 367mg;
Total Carbs: 5g; Fiber: 1g;
Protein: 15g

This makes a fine breakfast, for sure. But you may also want to keep it in mind for one of those evenings when you feel like serving breakfast for dinner. When you pull the pan out of the oven, the cheese is golden brown and gooey and the frittata is puffy and delicious.

3 tablespoons butter, divided

4 ounces button mushrooms, sliced

2 tablespoons minced shallot

½ teaspoon dried thyme

1 zucchini, ends cut flat and spiralized
    into spaghetti noodles

8 eggs

¼ cup heavy cream

½ teaspoon sea salt

¼ teaspoon freshly ground black pepper

1 teaspoon garlic powder

¼ cup shredded Swiss cheese

1. In a nonstick, ovenproof sauté pan, melt 2 tablespoons of the butter over medium-high heat.

2. Add the mushrooms, shallot, and thyme, and cook, stirring occasionally, until mushrooms are browned, about 5 minutes.

3. Remove the mushrooms from the pan with a slotted spoon and set them aside.

4. Add the remaining tablespoon of butter to the pan. Add the zucchini noodles and cook, stirring occasionally, until soft. Return the mushrooms to the pan.

5. Preheat the broiler.

6. In a large bowl, whisk together the eggs, heavy cream, salt, pepper, and garlic powder. Carefully pour the mixture over the zucchini and mushrooms.

7. Cook over medium-high, without stirring, until the eggs begin to set, about 4 minutes.

8. Sprinkle the cheese over the top and put the pan under the broiler. Broil until the cheese melts and the top sets and is lightly browned and puffy, 3 to 5 minutes more.

9. Serve immediately.

CANADIAN BACON CUPS
WITH BAKED EGGS AND CUCUMBER SLAW

PREP TIME: 10 MINUTES / COOK TIME: 15 MINUTES

HAND-CRANK

- Shredder blade
- Blade D

HOURGLASS

- Thin-cutting blade

SERVES 4

GLUTEN-FREE,
PALEO-FRIENDLY

PER SERVING: Calories: 156;
Total Fat: 9g; Saturated Fat: 2g;
Cholesterol: 180mg;
Total Carbs: 7g; Fiber: 1g;
Protein: 12g

Make individual breakfast servings by creating cups to hold the baked eggs. The crisp acidity of the slaw on top contrasts with the richness of the egg yolk and the smoky sweetness of the bacon. These tasty little packages make a satisfying breakfast.

FOR THE EGGS

4 large slices Canadian bacon

4 eggs

Sea salt

Freshly ground black pepper

FOR THE SLAW

1 cucumber, peeled, ends cut flat, and spiralized into spaghetti noodles

1 carrot, peeled, ends cut flat, and spiralized into spaghetti noodles

2 tablespoons Garlic Aioli (page 229)

Zest and juice of ½ orange

½ teaspoon homemade Sriracha (page 228) or store-bought

½ teaspoon sea salt

TO MAKE THE EGGS

1. Preheat the oven to 375°F.

2. Line each of 4 nonstick muffin cups with a slice of Canadian bacon.

3. Crack an egg into each piece of bacon and sprinkle with salt and pepper.

4. Bake in the oven until the egg whites set, about 14 minutes.

TO MAKE THE SLAW

1. While the eggs cook, cut the cucumber and carrot noodles into 1-inch pieces and put them in a large bowl.

2. In a small bowl, whisk together the aioli, orange zest, orange juice, sriracha, and salt. Toss with the cucumber and carrots.

3. Transfer each bacon cup to a plate and top with the slaw, and serve.

Substitution tip: *If you prefer your slaw a little less spicy, reduce the sriracha or leave it out altogether.*

FRIED EGGS WITH CHEESY SWEET POTATOES

PREP TIME: 10 MINUTES / COOK TIME: 30 MINUTES

IDEAL FOR HAND-CRANK
SPIRALIZERS

- Shredder blade
- Blade D

SERVES 4

GLUTEN-FREE, VEGETARIAN

PER SERVING: Calories: 218;
Total Fat: 17g; Saturated Fat: 10g;
Cholesterol: 199mg;
Total Carbs: 63g; Fiber: 1g;
Protein: 10g

Spiralizer alternative: *If you
have an hourglass spiralizer,
replace the sweet potato with
4 large peeled carrots and use
the thin-cutting blade.*

*After you bake the sweet potato noodles, toss them with your
favorite cheese. You can replace the pepper Jack with Asiago or
Cheddar, for example. Top each serving of cheesy noodles with
a fried egg for a rich and satisfying breakfast.*

FOR THE SWEET POTATOES

1 sweet potato, peeled, ends cut flat,
    and spiralized into spaghetti noodles
1 tablespoon butter, melted
½ teaspoon sea salt
¼ teaspoon freshly ground black pepper
¼ cup grated pepper Jack cheese

FOR THE EGGS

2 tablespoons butter
4 eggs
Sea salt
Black pepper

TO MAKE THE SWEET POTATOES

1. Preheat the oven to 400°F.

2. Line a large baking sheet with parchment paper.

3. Cut the sweet potato noodles crosswise into manageable
pieces, about 2 to 3 inches long. In a large bowl, toss them
with the melted butter, salt, and pepper. Spread out the
noodles on the baking sheet.

4. Bake for 10 minutes. Stir the noodles and return them
to the oven for another 5 minutes.

5. Turn the oven off and top the potato noodles with the grated cheese. Return to the turned-off oven and allow the cheese to melt while you prepare the eggs.

TO MAKE THE EGGS

1. In a large nonstick sauté pan, heat the butter over medium-high. Carefully crack the eggs into the pan. Season them with salt and pepper.

2. Cook until the egg whites are opaque, about 4 minutes. Carefully flip the eggs and turn off the heat. Allow the eggs to continue to cook in the turned-off pan for another minute, until the bottom of the egg is set but the yolk is still runny.

3. Divide the sweet potatoes among four plates and top each serving with an egg.

SAUSAGE AND MUSHROOM GRAVY
ON ZUCCHINI AND ONION BISCUITS

PREP TIME: 4 MINUTES, PLUS 8 HOURS TO SOAK THE MUSHROOMS / COOK TIME: 20 MINUTES

HAND-CRANK
- Shredder blade
- Blade D

HOURGLASS
- Thin-cutting blade

SERVES 4

GLUTEN-FREE,
PALEO-FRIENDLY

PER SERVING: Calories: 377;
Total Fat: 21g; Saturated Fat: 8g;
Cholesterol: 99mg;
Total Carbs: 26g; Fiber: 7g;
Protein: 21g

Who says biscuits and gravy can't be low-carb? Zucchini and onion fritters serve as the biscuits for a delicious breakfast sausage gravy. Dried porcini mushrooms give the gravy a lot of flavor. Plan to soak the mushrooms in the meat stock overnight. The next morning, prepare the gravy while the biscuits cook.

FOR THE GRAVY

2 cups Basic Meat or Poultry Stock (page 225),
    made with chicken

2 ounces dried porcini mushrooms

2 tablespoons unsalted butter

8 ounces bulk breakfast sausage

½ onion, minced

8 ounces button mushrooms, sliced

1 teaspoon dried thyme

¼ cup arrowroot powder

¼ cup water

1 teaspoon sea salt

¼ teaspoon freshly ground black pepper

2 tablespoons heavy cream

FOR THE ZUCCHINI AND ONION BISCUITS

1 zucchini, ends cut flat and spiralized into
    spaghetti noodles

1 tablespoon plus ½ teaspoon sea salt, divided

½ onion, minced

½ cup almond meal flour

½ teaspoon baking powder

1 tablespoon heavy cream

1 egg, lightly beaten

¼ teaspoon freshly ground black pepper

1. The night before, in a small bowl combine the meat stock and porcini mushrooms and cover with plastic wrap. Allow the mushrooms to soak for 8 hours or overnight in the refrigerator. The next morning, remove the mushrooms from the stock with a slotted spoon, reserving the stock. Squeeze the liquid out of the mushrooms and chop them finely. Set aside the mushrooms and stock separately.

2. In a large sauté pan, melt the butter over medium-high heat. Add the sausage and cook, breaking it up with a wooden spoon, until browned, about 6 minutes. Remove the sausage from the pan and set aside.

3. Add the onion, button mushrooms, chopped porcini mushrooms, and thyme to the pan. Cook, stirring occasionally, until the vegetables are browned, about 5 minutes.

4. Add the reserved stock to the vegetables and bring it to a simmer.

5. In a small bowl, whisk together the arrowroot powder, water, salt, and pepper. Add it to the broth and vegetables, stirring until the gravy thickens.

6. Stir in the heavy cream and remove from the heat. Rewarm the gravy just before serving.

TO MAKE THE BISCUITS

1. Preheat the oven to 400°F.

2. Line a baking sheet with parchment paper.

CONTINUED

3. In a colander set over the sink, sprinkle the zucchini noodles with 1 tablespoon of the salt and allow it to sit for 30 minutes to draw out water.

4. Rinse the zucchini to remove the salt and pat dry with paper towels.

5. In a large bowl, combine the zucchini with the onion, almond meal flour, baking powder, heavy cream, egg, the remaining ½ teaspoon of salt, and pepper, mixing well.

6. Drop the mixture by the spoonful onto the prepared baking sheet. Bake until golden brown on top, about 10 minutes. Turn the biscuits over and bake on the other side for another 10 minutes.

7. Serve the zucchini biscuits with the warm gravy spooned over the top.

APPLE AND CABBAGE HASH
WITH POACHED EGG

PREP TIME: 15 MINUTES / COOK TIME: 15 MINUTES

IDEAL FOR HAND-CRANK
SPIRALIZERS

- Shredder blade
- Blade D

SERVES 2

GLUTEN-FREE,
PALEO-FRIENDLY,
VEGETARIAN

PER SERVING: Calories: 267;
Total Fat: 18g; Saturated Fat: 13g;
Cholesterol: 164mg;
Total Carbs: 22g; Fiber: 5g;
Protein: 7g

Spiralizer alternative: *An hour-glass spiralizer will not work for this recipe. Instead, roughly chop the cabbage and thinly slice the apple.*

Apples and cabbage are a delicious combination. The poached eggs on top run over the mixture, serving as a tasty dressing.

1 apple, stemmed, cored, ends cut flat, and
   spiralized into spaghetti noodles
2 tablespoons coconut oil
¼ medium green cabbage, cored, outer leaves
   removed, and spiralized into spaghetti noodles
½ red onion, finely chopped
1 teaspoon dried thyme
½ teaspoon sea salt
¼ teaspoon freshly ground black pepper
1 garlic clove, minced
1 tablespoon red wine vinegar
2 eggs

1. Cut the apple noodles into ½-inch pieces and set aside.

2. In a large sauté pan, heat the oil over medium-high heat until it shimmers. Add apple noodles, cabbage noodles, and red onion. Sprinkle with the dried thyme, salt, and pepper.

3. Cook, stirring occasionally, until the vegetables are soft and begin to brown, about 10 minutes. Add the garlic and cook, stirring constantly, for about 30 to 60 seconds.

4. While the vegetables cook, fill a medium pot half full with water, add the red wine vinegar, and bring it to a simmer.

5. Working one at a time, crack the eggs into a small bowl and slip each egg into the water. Cook for 4 minutes.

6. Divide the cabbage mixture between two plates. Remove the eggs from the water with a slotted spoon and carefully place one on top of each mound of hash. Serve immediately.

3

SNACKS & SIDES

SWEET AND SPICY DAIKON RADISH FRIES

PREP TIME: 10 MINUTES / COOK TIME: 30 MINUTES

HAND-CRANK

- Shredder blade
- Blade D

HOURGLASS

- Thin-cutting blade

SERVES 2

GLUTEN-FREE,
PALEO-FRIENDLY, VEGAN

PER SERVING: Calories: 176;
Total Fat: 14g; Saturated Fat: 12g;
Cholesterol: 0mg; Total Carbs: 13g;
Fiber: 5g; Protein: 2g

A daikon radish has a slightly peppery taste. Serve these crispy roasted daikon fries with homemade Ketchup (page 230).

1 daikon radish, peeled, ends cut flat,
   and spiralized into spaghetti noodles
2 tablespoons coconut oil, melted
1 teaspoon homemade Sriracha (page 228)
   or store-bought
1 teaspoon wheat-free tamari or coconut aminos
¼ teaspoon stevia
½ teaspoon grated peeled fresh ginger
1 garlic clove, minced
½ teaspoon sea salt

1. Preheat the oven to 475°F.

2. Line a baking sheet with parchment paper.

3. Cut the radish strands crosswise into manageable pieces, about 2 to 3 inches long. Put them in a large bowl.

4. In a small bowl, whisk together the coconut oil, sriracha, tamari, stevia, ginger, garlic, and salt.

5. Drizzle the mixture evenly over the daikon radish noodles and toss to combine.

6. Spread out the daikon in a single layer on the prepared baking sheet. Bake, stirring once or twice, until golden brown, 20 to 30 minutes.

SWEET, SOUR, AND SPICY RAW CUCUMBER NOODLES

PREP TIME: 10 MINUTES

HAND-CRANK
- Shredder blade
- Blade D

HOURGLASS
- Thin-cutting blade

SERVES 2

GLUTEN-FREE,
PALEO-FRIENDLY, VEGAN

PER SERVING: Calories: 209;
Total Fat: 17g; Saturated Fat: 2g;
Cholesterol: 0mg; Total Carbs: 14g;
Fiber: 2g; Protein: 2g

This raw vegan dish is crisp and refreshing. The rice vinegar brings a bright acidity to the spicy vinaigrette. Crispy cucumber noodles serve as a nice contrast, cooling down the heat from the chili oil. Look for chili oil on the same shelf as the Asian condiments in your grocery store or in an Asian market.

2 cucumbers, peeled, ends cut flat,
    and spiralized into spaghetti noodles
2 scallions (white and green parts), thinly sliced
2 tablespoons toasted sesame seeds
¼ cup olive oil
1 teaspoon sesame oil
½ teaspoon chili oil
2 tablespoons rice vinegar
½ teaspoon grated orange zest, plus
    1 tablespoon freshly squeezed orange juice
1 garlic clove, minced
½ teaspoon grated peeled fresh ginger
¼ teaspoon sea salt
¼ teaspoon stevia

1. Pat the cucumber noodles dry with paper towels to remove excess water.

2. In a large bowl, combine the cucumber, scallions, and sesame seeds.

3. In a small bowl, whisk together the olive oil, sesame oil, chili oil, vinegar, orange zest and juice, garlic, ginger, salt, and stevia.

4. Toss the cucumber salad with the vinaigrette and serve.

CURRIED SWEET POTATO CHIPS
WITH RAITA

PREP TIME: 10 MINUTES / COOK TIME: 15 MINUTES

CHIPS

IDEAL FOR HAND-CRANK SPIRALIZERS

- Straight blade
- Blade A

RAITA

HAND-CRANK

- Shredder blade
- Blade D

HOURGLASS

- Thin-cutting blade

SERVES 2

GLUTEN-FREE,
PALEO-FRIENDLY, VEGAN

PER SERVING: Calories: 240;
Total Fat: 16g; Saturated Fat: 13g;
Cholesterol: 0mg; Total Carbs: 10g;
Fiber: 2g; Protein: 4g

Spiralizer alternative: *An hour-glass spiralizer will not work for the sweet potato chips. Instead, thinly slice the potato with a mandoline or a sharp knife.*

The ribbon-cutting blade of the spiralizer makes these chips divinely thin. Some spiralizers will cut sweet potatoes into slices with this blade, while others will make them into long ribbons. If your spiralizer makes ribbons, cut them crosswise to make chips. Serve with the refreshing raita for dipping.

FOR THE CHIPS

1 sweet potato, peeled, ends cut flat,
    and spiralized into ribboned noodles

2 tablespoons coconut oil, melted

1 teaspoon curry powder

½ teaspoon sea salt

FOR THE RAITA

2 cups plain coconut milk yogurt

Juice of 1 lemon

1 cucumber, peeled, ends cut flat,
    and spiralized into spaghetti noodles

½ teaspoon sea salt

TO MAKE THE CHIPS

1. Preheat the oven to 400°F.

2. Line a large baking sheet with parchment paper.

3. In a large bowl, toss the sweet potato chips with the melted coconut oil, curry powder, and salt.

4. Spread out the sweet potato on the baking sheet and bake until the chips are crisp around the edges, about 15 minutes. Remove from the oven.

5. Cool the chips in the pan. As they cool, the centers will crisp. When completely cool, transfer to a bowl.

TO MAKE THE RAITA

1. In a medium bowl, whisk together the yogurt and lemon juice.

2. In a food processor, pulse the cucumber noodles until it resembles rice, about 10 one-second pulses. Set aside.

3. Stir it into the yogurt mixture along with the salt.

4. Dip the crispy chips into the raita and enjoy.

Substitution tip: *You can use any kind of spice blend you like on these chips. For example, replace the curry powder with ½ teaspoon of garlic powder and ½ teaspoon of Italian seasoning.*

BUTTERNUT SQUASH NOODLES
WITH BROWN BUTTER AND SAGE

PREP TIME: 10 MINUTES / COOK TIME: 10 MINUTES

 IDEAL FOR HAND-CRANK
SPIRALIZER
- Shredder blade
- Blade D

SERVES 4

GLUTEN-FREE,
PALEO-FRIENDLY,
VEGETARIAN

PER SERVING: Calories: 225;
Total Fat: 18g; Saturated Fat: 8g;
Cholesterol: 31mg;
Total Carbs: 17g; Fiber: 3g;
Protein: 2g

Spiralizer alternative: *If you
have an hourglass spiralizer,
replace the butternut squash
with 3 large carrots. Spiralize
using the thin-cutting blade.*

*In many Paleo plans, butter is acceptable as long as it either is
clarified or comes from grass-fed cows. Clarified butter won't
brown because it has no milk solids. Grass-fed butter, however,
works perfectly. The browned butter adds a deep, nutty flavor to
the butternut squash, while the sage adds a pungent earthiness.*

1 medium butternut squash, peeled, ends cut flat,
    and spiralized into spaghetti noodles
2 tablespoons olive oil
½ teaspoon sea salt
¼ teaspoon freshly ground black pepper
¼ cup unsalted butter
12 fresh sage leaves

1. Preheat the oven to 400°F.

2. Line a baking sheet with parchment paper.

3. In a large bowl, toss the squash noodles with the olive oil,
salt, and pepper.

4. Put the squash on the prepared baking sheet and bake
until it softens, 6 to 7 minutes. Remove the squash from the
oven and allow it to cool slightly.

5. Meanwhile, in a large sauté pan, melt the butter over
medium-high heat, swirling the pan frequently, until the
butter begins to brown and starts to smell nutty.

6. Add the sage leaves and cook, stirring constantly, until they are browned and fragrant, about 2 minutes.

7. Toss the squash noodles with the butter and serve immediately.

Cooking tip: *Butter turns from perfectly browned to burned quickly, and burned butter imparts an acrid flavor. So keep a careful eye on the butter. For best results, use a sauté pan with a white or silver bottom, so you can see the color change as it happens.*

GARLIC, OLIVE OIL, AND HERB ZOODLES

PREP TIME: 10 MINUTES / COOK TIME: 10 MINUTES

HAND-CRANK
- Shredder blade
- Blade D

HOURGLASS
- Thin-cutting blade

SERVES 2

GLUTEN-FREE,
PALEO-FRIENDLY, VEGAN

PER SERVING: Calories: 221;
Total Fat: 22g; Saturated Fat: 3g;
Cholesterol: 0mg; Total Carbs: 9g;
Fiber: 3g; Protein: 3g

Sometimes the simplest things are the most delicious. These zucchini noodles don't take a lot of work, but they make a delicious snack. Or serve them as a side dish with your favorite meat, poultry, or fish.

3 tablespoons olive oil

2 zucchini, ends cut flat and spiralized into spaghetti noodles

3 garlic cloves, minced

Zest of ½ lemon

Pinch crushed red pepper flakes

½ teaspoon sea salt

¼ teaspoon freshly ground black pepper

3 tablespoons chopped fresh flat-leaf parsley

1. In a large sauté pan, heat the olive oil over medium-high heat until it shimmers.

2. Add the zucchini noodles and cook, stirring occasionally, until they are soft, about 6 minutes.

3. Add the garlic, lemon zest, red pepper flakes, salt, and pepper and cook, stirring constantly, until the garlic is fragrant, 30 to 60 seconds.

4. Remove from the heat and stir in the parsley. Serve immediately.

SWEET POTATO RICE
WITH MEDITERRANEAN SPICES

PREP TIME: 10 MINUTES / COOK TIME: 10 MINUTES

IDEAL FOR HAND-CRANK
SPIRALIZERS

- Shredder blade
- Blade D

SERVES 2

GLUTEN-FREE,
PALEO-FRIENDLY, VEGAN

PER SERVING: Calories: 201;
Total Fat: 15g; Saturated Fat: 2g;
Cholesterol: 0mg; Total Carbs: 17g;
Fiber: 3g; Protein: 3g

Spiralizer alternative: *If you
have an hourglass spiralizer,
replace the sweet potato
with 3 large peeled carrots.
Spiralize using the thin-
cutting blade.*

*The potato's sweet and earthy notes contrast with the fragrant
Mediterranean spices in this delicious dish. Use it as a base for
lamb stew or serve it with a hearty bean dish. If you don't have
any homemade vegetable stock on hand, use a good-quality
stock from the grocery store.*

1 sweet potato, peeled, ends cut flat,
   and spiralized into spaghetti noodles
2 tablespoons olive oil
½ onion, minced
½ teaspoon ground cumin
½ teaspoon ground cinnamon
¼ teaspoon ground ginger
2 garlic cloves, minced
½ cup Basic Vegetable Stock (page 224)
   or store-bought

1. In a food processor, pulse the sweet potato noodles until
it resembles rice, about 20 one-second pulses. Set aside.

2. In a large sauté pan, heat the olive oil over medium-high
heat until it shimmers.

3. Add the onion, cumin, cinnamon, and ginger and cook,
stirring occasionally, until the onion is soft, about 5 minutes.

4. Add the garlic and cook, stirring constantly, until it is
fragrant, 30 to 60 seconds.

5. Stir in the sweet potato rice and vegetable stock. Cook,
stirring occasionally, until the sweet potatoes are soft, about
5 minutes.

ROASTED ROOT VEGETABLES AND SHALLOTS

PREP TIME: 15 MINUTES / COOK TIME: 30 MINUTES

IDEAL FOR HAND-CRANK SPIRALIZERS

- Shredder blade
- Blade D

SERVES 4

GLUTEN-FREE,
PALEO-FRIENDLY, VEGAN

PER SERVING: Calories: 133;
Total Fat: 7g; Saturated Fat: 1g;
Cholesterol: 0mg; Total Carbs: 16g;
Fiber: 3g; Protein: 2g

Spiralizer alternative: *An hour-glass spiralizer will not work for the sweet potato and celeriac. Instead, use a vegetable peeler to shave both vegetables into thin strips and cut the strips lengthwise into strands of spaghetti.*

These veggies make a perfect side dish for fall and winter meals. Slice the shallots very thin so they roast evenly with the rest.

1 sweet potato, peeled, ends cut flat,
  and spiralized into spaghetti noodles
1 celeriac, greens removed, peeled, ends cut flat,
  and spiralized into spaghetti noodles
1 carrot, peeled, ends cut flat,
  and spiralized into spaghetti noodles
1 shallot, thinly sliced
3 garlic cloves, thinly sliced
2 tablespoons olive oil
1 teaspoon chopped fresh thyme
½ teaspoon sea salt
¼ teaspoon freshly ground black pepper

1. Preheat the oven to 400°F.

2. In a large bowl, toss together the sweet potato, celeriac, and carrot noodles, plus the shallot, garlic, olive oil, thyme, salt, and pepper. Spread out the vegetables on a large baking sheet.

3. Roast the vegetables, stirring once or twice during cooking, until they begin to brown, about 30 minutes.

4. Serve immediately.

PICKLED CUCUMBER RIBBONS

PREP TIME: 15 MINUTES / COOK TIME: 5 MINUTES, PLUS 8 HOURS TO PICKLE

 IDEAL FOR HAND-CRANK
SPIRALIZERS

- Straight blade
- Blade A

SERVES 2

GLUTEN-FREE,
PALEO-FRIENDLY, VEGAN

PER SERVING: Calories: 105;
Total Fat: 0g; Saturated Fat: 0g;
Cholesterol: 0mg; Total Carbs: 15g;
Fiber: 2g; Protein: 2g

If you like dill pickles, then you'll love these thin cucumber ribbons. They work well as a salad by themselves, as a snack, or as a topping to add some acidity to your favorite dish. And since the ribbons are so thin, they pickle overnight.

2 cucumbers, ends cut flat,
    spiralized into ribboned noodles
4 garlic cloves, crushed
3 fresh dill sprigs
Pinch crushed red pepper flakes
2 cups red wine vinegar
1 cup water
2 tablespoons sea salt

1. Cut the cucumber noodles crosswise into 3-inch pieces and put them in a large heat-proof bowl. Add the garlic cloves, dill, and red pepper flakes.

2. In a medium saucepan, simmer the red wine vinegar and sea salt until the salt completely dissolves.

3. Pour the hot brine over the cucumber mixture. Allow to sit on the counter until it cools completely. Cover and refrigerate for 8 hours, or overnight.

4. Transfer the pickles and brine to a glass jar and store, covered, until you are ready to eat them.

> **Cooking tip:** *If you like a zestier pickle, add up to ½ teaspoon of crushed red pepper flakes. If you prefer a sweeter pickle, add up to ½ teaspoon of stevia.*

COLORFUL RICE PILAF

PREP TIME: 15 MINUTES / COOK TIME: 20 MINUTES

IDEAL FOR HAND-CRANK
SPIRALIZERS

- Shredder blade
- Blade D

SERVES 4

GLUTEN-FREE,
PALEO-FRIENDLY, VEGAN

PER SERVING: Calories: 114;
Total Fat: 7g; Saturated Fat: 1g;
Cholesterol: 0mg; Total Carbs: 12g;
Fiber: 3g; Protein: 2g

Spiralizer alternative: *If you do
not have a hand-crank spiralizer, use a vegetable peeler to
shave the vegetables into thin
strips and process until they
resemble rice.*

*With red beets, orange carrots, white celeriac, and green herbs,
this rice pilaf is as pretty to look at as it is tasty to eat. Feel free
to exchange any of the root vegetables for others, depending on
what is in season and locally available.*

2 large carrots, peeled, ends cut flat,
    and spiralized into spaghetti noodles
1 large beet, peeled, ends cut flat,
    and spiralized into spaghetti noodles
1 large celeriac, greens removed, peeled, ends
    cut flat, and spiralized into spaghetti noodles
2 tablespoons olive oil
½ red onion, minced
½ red bell pepper, seeded and minced
1 teaspoon sea salt
¼ teaspoon freshly ground black pepper
2 garlic cloves, minced
¼ cup Basic Vegetable Stock (page 224)
    or store-bought
3 tablespoons chopped fresh flat-leaf parsley

1. In a food processor, pulse the carrots noodles and celeriac
noodles until they resemble rice, about 20 one-second pulses.
Set aside. Process the beet noodles separately or they will
dye the other vegetables red, for about 10 one-second pulses.
Set aside.

2. In a large sauté pan, heat the olive oil over medium-high
heat until it shimmers. Add the onion, bell pepper, salt, and
pepper, and cook, stirring occasionally, until the onion is soft,
about 5 minutes.

3. Add the garlic and cook, stirring constantly, until it is fragrant, 30 to 60 seconds.

4. Add the vegetable stock, carrot rice, beet rice, and celeriac rice. Cook, stirring frequently, until the rice is soft, 3 to 4 minutes.

5. Stir in the parsley and serve hot.

SWEET POTATO GRATIN

PREP TIME: 15 MINUTES / COOK TIME: 50 MINUTES

IDEAL FOR HAND-CRANK SPIRALIZERS

- Straight blade
- Blade A

SERVES 8

GLUTEN-FREE, VEGETARIAN

PER SERVING: Calories: 174; Total Fat: 8g; Saturated Fat: 5g; Cholesterol: 26mg; Total Carbs: 22g; Fiber: 3g; Protein: 3g

---

Spiralizer alternative: *An hourglass spiralizer will not work for this recipe. Instead, use a mandoline or a sharp knife to cut the sweet potato.*

Reserve this rich gratin, with its creamy sauce, for those special occasions when you want to serve a more decadent side dish. Use the ribbon blade of the spiralizer. If your blade slices the sweet potatoes, then you don't need to do anymore. If you get ribbons, you'll need to cut them crosswise into slices.

2 tablespoons unsalted butter

1 shallot, minced

2 sweet potatoes, peeled, ends cut flat, and spiralized into ribboned noodles

1 teaspoon chopped fresh thyme

½ teaspoon sea salt

¼ teaspoon freshly ground black pepper

¾ cup finely grated Asiago cheese, divided

¾ cup heavy cream

1¼ cups Basic Vegetable Stock (page 224) or store-bought

1. Preheat the oven to 400°F.

2. In a large, ovenproof skillet, melt the butter over medium-high heat. Add the shallot and cook, stirring occasionally, until soft, about 4 minutes.

3. Scrape the shallot and butter into a large bowl. Then add the sweet potato ribbons, thyme, salt, pepper, and ½ cup of the cheese. Mix well and put the mixture back in the skillet.

4. In a small bowl, mix together the heavy cream and vegetable stock. Pour it over the potato mixture in the skillet.

5. Sprinkle the remaining ¼ cup of cheese over the top.

6. Put the skillet in the oven and bake until the potatoes absorb the cream and are tender, about 45 minutes. Cool for 15 minutes before serving.

Make it lighter: *If you don't have (or want to use) heavy cream, you can use almond milk or 2% milk. If you use either of these, eliminate the vegetable stock and instead use 2 cups of the milk.*

4

SALADS

SPICY AVOCADO ORANGE SLAW

PREP TIME: 10 MINUTES

IDEAL FOR HAND-CRANK
SPIRALIZERS

- Shredder blade
- Blade D

SERVES 4

GLUTEN-FREE,
PALEO-FRIENDLY, VEGAN

PER SERVING: Calories: 201;
Total Fat: 17g; Saturated Fat: 3g;
Cholesterol: 0mg; Total Carbs: 13g;
Fiber: 6g; Protein: 3g

Spiralizer alternative: *An hour-glass spiralizer isn't well suited to make cabbage noodles. Instead, shred the cabbage by grating it on the large holes of a box grater or cutting it into shreds with a sharp knife.*

Creamy avocado replaces mayonnaise in this tasty slaw. The avocado adds grassy and slightly sweet notes to an acidic and spicy dressing. Meanwhile, the cabbage and carrots offer a satisfyingly crispy crunch.

1 carrot, peeled, ends cut flat,
    and spiralized into spaghetti noodles
½ medium cabbage, cored, outer leaves
    removed, and spiralized into spaghetti noodles
3 scallions (white and green parts), thinly sliced
1 avocado, pitted and peeled
3 tablespoons apple cider vinegar
Zest of ½ orange, plus juice of 1 orange
2 garlic cloves, minced
2 tablespoons olive oil
1 teaspoon homemade Sriracha (page 228)
    or store-bought
½ teaspoon sea salt
¼ teaspoon freshly ground black pepper

1. Cut the carrot noodles into 2-inch pieces. Put them in a large bowl and add the cabbage noodles and scallions.

2. In a blender or food processor, combine the avocado, apple cider vinegar, orange zest and juice, garlic cloves, olive oil, sriracha, salt, and pepper. Blend until smooth and well combined.

3. Toss the slaw with the dressing.

CUCUMBER AND STRAWBERRY SALAD
WITH ORANGE VINAIGRETTE

PREP TIME: 10 MINUTES

HAND-CRANK
- Shredder blade
- Blade D

HOURGLASS
- Thin-cutting blade

SERVES 4

GLUTEN-FREE,
PALEO-FRIENDLY, VEGAN

PER SERVING: Calories: 171;
Total Fat: 13g; Saturated Fat: 2g;
Cholesterol: 0mg; Total Carbs: 15g;
Fiber: 3g; Protein: 2g

Strawberries are relatively low in sugar, which makes them ideal for reduced-carbohydrate recipes. The combination of sweet sliced strawberries, refreshing cucumber noodles, and a citrusy vinaigrette makes for a tasty, light salad. Serve it in early summer, when strawberries are in season.

2 cucumbers, peeled, ends cut flat,
   and spiralized into spaghetti noodles
1 pint strawberries, sliced and hulled
2 cups baby spinach
Zest of ½ orange, plus juice of 1 orange
1 tablespoon apple cider vinegar
¼ cup olive oil
½ teaspoon chopped fresh thyme
½ teaspoon sea salt
¼ freshly ground black pepper

1. Pat the cucumber noodles dry with a paper towel and put them in a large bowl. Add the strawberries and spinach.

2. In a small bowl, whisk together the orange zest and juice, apple cider vinegar, olive oil, thyme, salt, and pepper.

3. Toss the salad with the vinaigrette, or serve the salad with the vinaigrette on the side for drizzling.

CARROT, FENNEL, AND APPLE SALAD

PREP TIME: 10 MINUTES

IDEAL FOR HAND-CRANK SPIRALIZERS

- Shredder blade
- Blade D

SERVES 4

GLUTEN-FREE, PALEO-FRIENDLY, VEGAN

PER SERVING: Calories: 270; Total Fat: 26g; Saturated Fat: 4g; Cholesterol: 0mg; Total Carbs: 13g; Fiber: 4g; Protein: 1g

---

Spiralizer alternative: *If you have an hourglass spiralizer, use a vegetable peeler to cut the apple into thin strips. Then use a sharp knife to cut strips into narrow noodles. Your spiralizer should work well to make the carrot noodles using the thin-cutting blade.*

This salad is really easy to make and so crispy and refreshing. A touch of ginger in a simple, lemon-based vinaigrette adds a little bit of spice.

1 apple, stemmed, cored, ends cut flat, and spiralized into spaghetti noodles

1 large carrot, peeled, ends cut flat, and spiralized into spaghetti noodles

1 fennel bulb, shaved (see Cooking tip), plus 1 teaspoon chopped fennel fronds

½ cup olive oil

Zest of 1 lemon, plus juice of 2 lemons

½ teaspoon grated peeled fresh ginger

½ teaspoon sea salt

¼ teaspoon freshly ground black pepper

1. In a large bowl, combine the noodles with the shaved fennel.

2. In a small bowl, whisk together the olive oil, lemon zest and juice, ginger, salt, pepper, and fennel fronds.

3. Toss the salad with the vinaigrette, or serve it on the side for drizzling.

> **Cooking tip:** *Fennel bulbs come with stalks and fronds. Remove them, setting aside a few fronds for the vinaigrette. Clean the fennel bulb, and use a mandoline or vegetable peeler to create thin shavings.*

MEDITERRANEAN SALAD
WITH OREGANO–BASIL VINAIGRETTE

PREP TIME: 10 MINUTES

HAND-CRANK
- Shredder blade
- Blade D

HOURGLASS
- Thin-cutting blade

SERVES 4

GLUTEN-FREE,
PALEO-FRIENDLY,
VEGETARIAN

PER SERVING: Calories: 351;
Total Fat: 33g; Saturated Fat: 7g;
Cholesterol: 17mg;
Total Carbs: 13g; Fiber: 3g;
Protein: 5g

This refreshing salad brings the taste of the Mediterranean home with crunchy cucumbers, juicy tomatoes, and salty olives and feta cheese. Choose juicy cherry tomatoes that are at their peak, because their sweetness will enhance the salad. You can replace the kalamata olives with black olives, if you like.

2 cucumbers, peeled, ends cut flat,
    and spiralized into spaghetti noodles
1 cup cherry tomatoes, halved
1 cup kalamata olives, pitted and halved
½ red onion, thinly sliced
½ cup crumbled feta
½ cup olive oil
Zest of ½ lemon, plus juice of 1 lemon
3 tablespoons red wine vinegar
2 garlic cloves, finely minced
1 tablespoon chopped fresh basil
1 tablespoon chopped fresh oregano
½ teaspoon sea salt
¼ teaspoon freshly ground black pepper

1. Pat the zucchini noodles dry with paper towels and put them in a large bowl. Add the cherry tomatoes, olives, red onion, and feta.

2. In a small bowl, whisk together the olive oil, lemon zest and juice, red wine vinegar, garlic, basil, oregano, salt, and pepper.

3. Toss the salad with the vinaigrette, or serve the vinaigrette on the side for drizzling.

BROCCOLI SLAW
WITH CREAMY LEMON–HERB DRESSING
AND SLIVERED ALMONDS

PREP TIME: 10 MINUTES

 HAND-CRANK
- Shredder blade
- Blade D

 HOURGLASS
- Thin-cutting blade

SERVES 4

GLUTEN-FREE,
PALEO-FRIENDLY,
VEGETARIAN

PER SERVING: Calories: 343;
Total Fat: 26g; Saturated Fat: 3g;
Cholesterol: 15mg;
Total Carbs: 26g; Fiber: 5g;
Protein: 6g

Spiralizer alternative: *If the
broccoli stems are too thin for
your hand-crank spiralizer, use a
vegetable peeler to shave them
into thin strips. With a sharp
knife, cut the strips lengthwise
into narrow noodles.*

*Broccoli stems spiralize quite well, especially in an hourglass
spiralizer. Chop off the large, thick stems to spiralize, and then
trim away the heads of the broccoli and break them into small
florets to toss with the salad.*

2 cups broccoli stems, spiralized into spaghetti
    noodles, plus 2 cups broccoli florets
1 large carrot, peeled, ends cut flat,
    and spiralized into spaghetti noodles
½ cup slivered almonds
1 cup Garlic Aioli (page 229)
Zest of ½ lemon, plus juice of 1 lemon
1 teaspoon chopped fresh rosemary
1 tablespoon chopped fresh thyme
1 tablespoon chopped fresh chives
½ teaspoon sea salt
¼ teaspoon freshly ground black pepper

1. Cut the broccoli and carrot noodles into 2-inch pieces.
Put them in a large bowl and add the broccoli florets
and almonds.

2. In a small bowl, whisk together the aioli, lemon zest
and juice, rosemary, thyme, chives, salt, and pepper.

3. Toss the salad with the dressing.

BEET AND ARUGULA SALAD
WITH GOAT CHEESE AND WALNUTS

PREP TIME: 10 MINUTES

IDEAL FOR HAND-CRANK
SPIRALIZERS
- Shredder blade
- Blade D

SERVES 4

GLUTEN-FREE,
PALEO-FRIENDLY,
VEGETARIAN

PER SERVING: Calories: 380;
Total Fat: 34g; Saturated Fat: 7g;
Cholesterol: 17mg;
Total Carbs: 16g; Fiber: 4g;
Protein: 7g

The slightly bitter, peppery bite of baby arugula provides a perfect contrast to the sweet, earthy beets. The combination of the ruby-colored beets and the greens also makes this a visually appealing salad. What makes this recipe ideal for a hand-crank spiralizer is that it calls for spiralized beets, which the hourglass spiralizer can't tackle. If you have an hourglass spiralizer, replace the beets with cucumber and spiralize with the thin-cutting blade.

1 pound beets, peeled, ends cut flat,
    and spiralized into spaghetti noodles
1 carrot, peeled, ends cut flat,
    and spiralized into spaghetti noodles
2 cups baby arugula
1 shallot, thinly sliced
½ cup goat cheese
¼ cup walnut pieces
½ cup olive oil
3 tablespoons balsamic vinegar
1 teaspoon Dijon mustard
2 tablespoons chopped fresh tarragon
½ teaspoon sea salt
¼ teaspoon freshly ground black pepper

1. In a large bowl, combine the beet noodles, carrot noodles, baby arugula, shallot, goat cheese, and walnuts.

2. In a small bowl, whisk together the olive oil, vinegar, mustard, tarragon, salt, and pepper.

3. Toss the dressing with the salad, or serve it on the side for drizzling.

APPLE, PEAR, AND SPINACH SALAD
WITH GINGER VINAIGRETTE

PREP TIME: 10 MINUTES

 IDEAL FOR HAND-CRANK
SPIRALIZERS
- Shredder blade
- Blade D

SERVES 4

GLUTEN-FREE,
PALEO-FRIENDLY, VEGAN

PER SERVING: Calories: 250;
Total Fat: 16g; Saturated Fat: 3g;
Cholesterol: 0mg; Total Carbs: 27g;
Fiber: 7g; Protein: 2g

Spiralizer alternative: *If you
have an hourglass spiralizer,
use a vegetable peeler to cut
the apple and pear into thin
strips. Then use a sharp knife
to cut strips lengthwise into
narrow noodles.*

Crispy apples and juicy pears provide a fresh and fruity contrast to the baby spinach. The minced fresh ginger in the vinaigrette complements the apples and pears perfectly.

1 apple, stemmed, cored, ends cut flat,
    and spiralized into spaghetti noodles
1 pear, stemmed, ends cut flat, and spiralized
    into spaghetti noodles
½ medium jicama, peeled, ends cut flat,
    and spiralized into spaghetti noodles
3 cups baby spinach
2 tablespoons balsamic vinegar
Zest of ½ orange, plus 1 tablespoon freshly
    squeezed orange juice
¼ cup olive oil
½ teaspoon freshly grated peeled ginger
½ teaspoon sea salt
¼ teaspoon freshly ground black pepper

1. In a large bowl, toss together the apple, pear, and jicama noodles, and then combine with the baby spinach.

2. In a small bowl, whisk together the balsamic vinegar, orange zest and juice, olive oil, ginger, salt, and pepper.

3. Toss the salad with the vinaigrette, or serve it on the side for drizzling.

> **Substitution tip:** *For a tart and tangy
> flavor, use lime zest and juice in the
> vinaigrette with 2 tablespoons of
> chopped cilantro.*

JICAMA, SCALLION, AND TOMATO SALAD
WITH AVOCADO–LIME–CILANTRO VINAIGRETTE

PREP TIME: 10 MINUTES

IDEAL FOR HAND-CRANK SPIRALIZERS

- Shredder blade
- Blade D

SERVES 4

GLUTEN-FREE,
PALEO-FRIENDLY, VEGAN

PER SERVING: Calories: 284;
Total Fat: 21g; Saturated Fat: 4g;
Cholesterol: 0mg; Total Carbs: 24g;
Fiber: 11g; Protein: 3g

This salad is wonderful as is, but you can make it into a main course by adding some chopped rotisserie chicken for added protein. Tomatoes are best when they're in season during the summer months. Look for ripe heirloom tomatoes at your local farmers' market.

1 medium jicama, peeled, ends cut flat,
    and spiralized into spaghetti noodles
6 scallions (white and green parts), thinly sliced
2 large heirloom tomatoes, chopped
2 tablespoons apple cider vinegar
1 teaspoon Dijon mustard
¼ cup olive oil
½ teaspoon sea salt
¼ teaspoon freshly ground black pepper
½ avocado, peeled and pitted
Grated zest of 1 lime, plus juice of 2 limes
1 garlic clove, minced
3 tablespoons chopped fresh cilantro

1. In a large bowl, combine the jicama noodles, scallions, and tomatoes.

2. In a blender or food processor, combine the apple cider vinegar, Dijon mustard, olive oil, salt, pepper, avocado, lime zest and juice, garlic, and cilantro. Blend until smooth.

3. Toss the salad with the dressing, or serve the dressing on the side for drizzling.

CARROT AND KALE SALAD
WITH PINE NUTS

PREP TIME: 10 MINUTES

 HAND-CRANK
- Shredder blade
- Blade D

HOURGLASS
- Thin-cutting blade

SERVES 4

GLUTEN-FREE,
PALEO-FRIENDLY, VEGAN

PER SERVING: Calories: 254;
Total Fat: 22g; Saturated Fat: 3g;
Cholesterol: 0mg; Total Carbs: 14g;
Fiber: 2g; Protein: 4g

With a deliciously sweet orange vinaigrette, humble kale and carrots are elevated into a scrumptious salad that makes a great main dish or side. This is also a very healthy salad. Kale is loaded with antioxidants and fiber, which is why it's considered a superfood.

FOR THE SALAD

2 large carrots, peeled, ends cut flat,
    and spiralized into spaghetti noodles
4 cups torn deribbed kale
¼ cup pine nuts

FOR THE VINAIGRETTE

3 tablespoons balsamic vinegar
1 teaspoon Dijon mustard
¼ cup olive oil
½ teaspoon sea salt
¼ teaspoon freshly ground black pepper
Zest and juice of 1 orange
¼ teaspoon homemade Sriracha (page 228)
    or store-bought
1 garlic clove, minced

1. Cut the carrot noodles crosswise into 2-inch pieces. Put them in a large bowl and add the kale and pine nuts.

2. In a small bowl, whisk together the balsamic vinegar, Dijon mustard, olive oil, salt, pepper, orange zest and juice, sriracha, and garlic.

3. Toss the salad with the vinaigrette, or serve it on the side for drizzling.

CREAMY CHICKEN SALAD
WITH CARROTS, BROCCOLI, AND RED BELL PEPPER

PREP TIME: 10 MINUTES

 IDEAL FOR HAND-CRANK
SPIRALIZERS
- Straight blade
- Blade A

SERVES 4

GLUTEN-FREE,
PALEO-FRIENDLY

PER SERVING: Calories: 313;
Total Fat: 11g; Saturated Fat: 3g;
Cholesterol: 125mg;
Total Carbs: 10g; Fiber: 3g;
Protein: 43g

Spiralizer alternative: *Although
this recipe is written with carrot
ribbons in mind, there's no
crime in making fettuccine
noodles if you only have an
hourglass-shaped spiralizer.
The thick-cutting blade will do
the trick.*

*Save time by using rotisserie chicken, which you can buy at the
grocery store. Remove the skin and use a combination of white
and dark meat. This recipe travels well, so it's a great salad to
take to work for lunch.*

2 large carrots, peeled, ends cut flat,
    and spiralized into ribboned noodles
1 cup broccoli florets
1 red bell pepper, seeded and cut
    into matchsticks
½ fennel bulb, shaved with vegetable peeler
    or mandoline
2 scallions (white and green parts), thinly sliced
4 cups chopped cooked chicken
½ cup Garlic Aioli (page 229)
Grated zest of ½ lemon, plus 1 tablespoon freshly
    squeezed lemon juice
2 tablespoons chopped fresh tarragon
½ teaspoon sea salt
¼ teaspoon freshly ground black pepper

1. Cut the carrot ribbons crosswise into 2-inch pieces.
Put them in a large bowl and add the broccoli, bell pepper,
fennel, scallions, and chicken.

2. In a small bowl, whisk together the aioli, lemon zest
and juice, tarragon, salt, and pepper.

3. Toss the salad with the dressing and serve.

5

SOUPS & STEWS

MISO SOUP
WITH SWEET POTATO RAMEN

PREP TIME: 10 MINUTES / COOK TIME: 15 MINUTES

IDEAL FOR HAND-CRANK
SPIRALIZERS
- Shredder blade
- Blade D

SERVES 4

GLUTEN-FREE, VEGAN

PER SERVING: Calories: 216;
Total Fat: 10g; Saturated Fat: 7g;
Cholesterol: 0mg; Total Carbs: 22g;
Fiber: 4g; Protein: 11g

Spiralizer alternative: *An hourglass spiralizer will not work
for the sweet potato. Instead,
thinly slice the potato with a
mandoline or a sharp knife.*

*In this soup, miso and shiitake mushrooms provide the umami,
a deep savoriness. The mushrooms balance the sweet earthiness of the potatoes. With warm, spicy, and savory Asian
flavors, this soup is a perfect vegetarian lunch or dinner.*

2 tablespoons coconut oil
6 scallions (white and green parts), thinly sliced
8 ounces shiitake mushrooms,
    stemmed and sliced
2 garlic cloves, minced
6 cups Basic Vegetable Stock (page 224)
    or store-bought
3 tablespoons gluten-free miso paste
Dash crushed red pepper flakes
1 cup chopped kale, ribs removed
1 sweet potato, peeled, ends cut flat,
    and spiralized into spaghetti noodles

1. In a large pot, heat the coconut oil over medium-high heat
until it shimmers.

2. Add the scallions and mushrooms and cook, stirring occasionally, until the mushrooms are soft, about 5 minutes.

3. Add the garlic and cook, stirring constantly, until it is
fragrant, 30 to 60 seconds.

4. Add the vegetable stock, miso, and red pepper flakes.
Bring the soup to a boil.

5. Add the kale and sweet potato. Reduce the heat to
medium and simmer until the noodles are al dente, 5 to
10 minutes more.

AVGOLEMONO SOUP
WITH JICAMA RICE

PREP TIME: 10 MINUTES / COOK TIME: 10 MINUTES

IDEAL FOR HAND-CRANK
SPIRALIZERS

- Shredder blade
- Blade D

SERVES 4

GLUTEN-FREE,
PALEO-FRIENDLY

PER SERVING: Calories: 245;
Total Fat: 6g; Saturated Fat: 2g;
Cholesterol: 147mg;
Total Carbs: 17g; Fiber: 8g;
Protein: 30g

Spiralizer alternative: *If you
have an hourglass spiralizer,
you can replace the jicama
with 2 large, peeled carrots. To
make this vegetarian, leave out
the chicken and replace the
meat stock with Basic Vegetable Stock (page 224).*

*This traditional egg and lemon broth soup is a classic
Mediterranean (specifically Greek) dish. The soup is typically
made with either orzo or rice. To save carbs and make it gluten-
free, however, here it is made with riced jicama.*

1 medium jicama, peeled, ends cut flat,
    and spiralized into spaghetti noodles
6 cups Basic Meat or Poultry Stock (page 225),
    made with chicken
½ teaspoon sea salt
¼ teaspoon freshly ground black pepper
12 ounces cooked chicken, cut into pieces
½ cup lemon juice, freshly squeezed
2 eggs

1. In a food processor, pulse the jicama noodles until it
resembles rice, 10 to 20 one-second pulses.

2. In a large pot, combine the jicama rice with the
chicken stock, salt, and pepper. Bring it to a simmer over
medium-high heat and simmer until the jicama is al dente,
5 to 10 minutes.

3. Add the chicken and simmer an additional 2 to 3 minutes.

4. In a small bowl, whisk together the lemon juice and the
eggs. Add this mixture to the soup in a thin stream, whisking
constantly. Serve hot.

COCONUT, GINGER, AND SHIITAKE SOUP
WITH CUCUMBER NOODLES

PREP TIME: 10 MINUTES / COOK TIME: 20 MINUTES

 HAND-CRANK

- Shredder blade
- Blade D

HOURGLASS

- Thin-cutting blade

SERVES 4

GLUTEN-FREE,
PALEO-FRIENDLY, VEGAN

PER SERVING: Calories: 398;
Total Fat: 33g; Saturated Fat: 29g;
Cholesterol: 0mg; Total Carbs: 23g;
Fiber: 5g; Protein: 8g

Who needs meat when you have mushrooms? Shiitake mushrooms are dense and toothsome, so they add heartiness and flavor to this Asian-inspired soup. The creamy coconut broth combines with a hint of lime for richness and acidity.

2 tablespoons coconut oil

½ onion, minced

8 ounces shiitake mushrooms,
    stemmed and sliced

3 garlic cloves, finely minced

1 teaspoon grated ginger

3 cups Basic Vegetable Stock (page 224)
    or store-bought

1 (15-ounce) can full-fat coconut milk

Juice of 2 limes

½ teaspoon sea salt

½ teaspoon homemade Sriracha (page 228)
    or store-bought

1 cucumber, ends cut flat and spiralized
    into spaghetti noodles

1 large carrot, peeled, ends cut flat, and
    spiralized into spaghetti noodles

3 tablespoons chopped fresh cilantro

1. In a large pot, heat the coconut oil over medium-high heat until it shimmers.

2. Add the onion and mushrooms and cook, stirring occasionally, until vegetables are soft, about 5 minutes.

3. Add the garlic and ginger and cook, stirring constantly, until garlic is fragrant, 30 to 60 seconds.

4. Stir in the vegetable stock, coconut milk, lime juice, salt, and sriracha, and bring it to a simmer.

5. Add the cucumber and carrot noodles and cook until they are al dente, about 5 minutes more.

6. Stir in the cilantro and serve.

THAI BEEF ZOODLE SOUP

PREP TIME: 15 MINUTES / COOK TIME: 20 MINUTES

 HAND-CRANK
- Shredder blade
- Blade D

HOURGLASS
- Thin-cutting blade

SERVES 4

GLUTEN-FREE,
PALEO-FRIENDLY

PER SERVING: Calories: 350;
Total Fat: 17g; Saturated Fat: 10g;
Cholesterol: 62mg;
Total Carbs: 10g; Fiber: 3g;
Protein: 39g

This fragrant soup uses beef, so it's nice and hearty. Use a beef that stays tender when cooked over high heat, such as flank steak. Cut the steak strips against the grain to shorten the fibers, keeping it tender. To make this Paleo-friendly, use Red Boat fish sauce.

2 tablespoons coconut oil

1 pound flank steak, cut against the grain
    into quarter-inch thick strips

4 scallions (white and green parts), thinly sliced

2 celery stalks, thinly sliced

1 carrot, peeled and thinly sliced

6 garlic cloves, thinly sliced

6 cups Basic Meat or Poultry Stock (page 225),
    made with beef

1 tablespoon fish sauce

½ teaspoon ground cinnamon

½ teaspoon freshly ground black pepper

½ teaspoon homemade Sriracha (page 228)
    or store-bought

3 zucchini, ends cut flat and spiralized into
    spaghetti noodles

3 tablespoons chopped fresh cilantro

1. In a large pot, heat the coconut oil over medium-high heat until it shimmers.

2. Add the flank steak and cook, stirring occasionally, until it is browned, about 6 minutes. Remove the steak from the oil with a slotted spoon and set it aside on a platter.

3. Add the scallions, celery, and carrot to the pot and cook, stirring occasionally, until the vegetables are soft, about 5 minutes.

4. Add the garlic and cook, stirring constantly, until it is fragrant, 30 to 60 seconds.

5. Add the meat stock, fish sauce, cinnamon, pepper, and sriracha to the pot. Bring the soup to a simmer.

6. Add the zucchini noodles to the pot. Simmer until the noodles are al dente, about 5 minutes.

7. Return the reserved beef to the pot and simmer for 1 minute.

8. Stir in the cilantro and serve immediately.

Make it lighter: *To make this vegan, eliminate the beef and replace it with 8 ounces of cubed tofu. Replace the beef stock with the Basic Vegetable Stock (page 224) and cut out the fish sauce.*

ITALIAN SAUSAGE, FENNEL, AND MUSHROOM SOUP

PREP TIME: 10 MINUTES / COOK TIME: 20 MINUTES

 HAND-CRANK

- Shredder blade
- Blade D

HOURGLASS

- Thin-cutting blade

SERVES 4

GLUTEN-FREE,
PALEO-FRIENDLY

PER SERVING: Calories: 442;
Total Fat: 32g; Saturated Fat: 9g;
Cholesterol: 71mg;
Total Carbs: 15g; Fiber: 4g;
Protein: 24g

Use bulk Italian sausage—that is, sausage without casings— for this tasty soup. If you can't find Italian sausage in bulk, then buy regular Italian sausage and remove the casings by running a sharp knife diagonally across the sausage and squeezing the meat from the casing. For a spicier soup, choose hot Italian sausage.

2 carrots, peeled, ends cut flat, and spiralized
    into spaghetti noodles

1 zucchini, peeled, ends cut flat, and spiralized
    into spaghetti noodles

2 tablespoons olive oil

12 ounces bulk Italian sausage

1 onion, chopped

8 ounces crimini mushrooms, sliced

1 fennel bulb, thinly sliced

3 garlic cloves, minced

6 cups Basic Meat or Poultry Stock (page 225),
    beef or chicken

¼ teaspoon sea salt

¼ teaspoon fresh ground black pepper

1. After spiralizing, cut the carrot and zucchini noodles into elbow shapes to make macaroni. Set aside.

2. In a large pot, heat the olive oil over medium-high heat until it shimmers. Add the sausage and cook, crumbling with a spoon, until it is browned, about 6 minutes. Remove the sausage from the oil with a slotted spoon and set it aside on a platter.

3. To the oil that remains in the pan, add the onion, mushrooms, and fennel. Cook, stirring occasionally, until the vegetables soften, 5 to 7 minutes.

4. Add the garlic and cook, stirring constantly, until it is fragrant, 30 to 60 seconds.

5. Add the broth, scraping up any browned bits from the bottom of the pan with the side of the spoon. Return the sausage to the pan and add the zucchini and carrot macaroni.

6. Simmer until the macaroni is al dente, about 5 minutes.

TOM GA GAI
WITH QUICK PICKLED CUCUMBER NOODLES

PREP TIME: 10 MINUTES PLUS OVERNIGHT REFRIGERATION / COOK TIME: 20 MINUTES

HAND-CRANK
- Shredder blade
- Blade D

HOURGLASS
- Thin-cutting blade

SERVES 4

GLUTEN-FREE,
PALEO-FRIENDLY

PER SERVING: Calories: 440;
Total Fat: 28g; Saturated Fat: 21g;
Cholesterol: 73mg;
Total Carbs: 15g; Fiber: 3g;
Protein: 36g

Tom ga gai is a Thai coconut and chicken soup. The quick pickled cucumber noodles are added at the end as a garnish to the soup, cutting through the fatty richness of the coconut milk with a crisp acidity that lends balance to the dish. Make the noodles the night before so they have time to soak up the brine.

FOR THE CUCUMBER NOODLES

1 cucumber, peeled, ends cut flat,
    and spiralized into spaghetti noodles

1 cup rice vinegar

1 cup water

½ teaspoon stevia

3 teaspoons sea salt

FOR THE SOUP

1 (14-ounce) can coconut milk

4 cups Basic Meat or Poultry Stock (page 225),
    made with chicken

5 half-inch thick slices of peeled ginger

Zest of 1 lemon

12 ounces boneless, skinless chicken breast,
    cut into 1-inch cubes

1 cup sliced shiitake mushrooms

1 tablespoon fish sauce

1 teaspoon homemade Sriracha (page 228)
    or store-bought

2 tablespoons chopped fresh cilantro

1. In a small saucepan, bring the vinegar, water, stevia, and salt to a simmer. Cook until the salt dissolves completely.

2. In a large bowl, pour the vinegar mixture over the cucumber noodles. Allow to cool for 30 minutes. Remove the noodles from the brine and put them in a sealable container. Refrigerate overnight or for up to one month.

TO MAKE THE SOUP

1. In a large pot, bring the coconut milk, stock, ginger, and lemon zest to a simmer over medium-high heat.

2. Add the chicken, mushrooms, fish sauce, and sriracha. Simmer until the chicken cooks through, 5 to 10 minutes.

3. Remove the ginger pieces.

4. Stir in the cilantro.

5. Remove the cucumber noodles from the brine and put them on top of the soup as a garnish.

> **Make it lighter:** *To make this vegetarian, replace the chicken stock with Basic Vegetable Stock (page 224). Eliminate the chicken and instead use 8 ounces of cubed tofu. Eliminate the fish sauce and instead use 1 tablespoon of soy sauce (or coconut aminos if you prefer gluten-free).*

BEEFARONI
WITH CARAMELIZED ONIONS

PREP TIME: 10 MINUTES / COOK TIME: 40 MINUTES

HAND-CRANK

- Shredder blade
- Blade D

HOURGLASS

- Thin-cutting blade

SERVES 4

GLUTEN-FREE,
PALEO-FRIENDLY

PER SERVING: Calories: 301;
Total Fat: 13g; Saturated Fat: 3g;
Cholesterol: 76mg;
Total Carbs: 17g; Fiber: 5g;
Protein: 30g

Beefaroni doesn't have to be high in carbs. Replace the macaroni with healthy, high-fiber carrots. Caramelized onions elevate this Beefaroni, adding rich and slightly sweet flavors to the dish. Choose organic ground beef that has at least 15 percent fat (85 percent lean).

3 large carrots, peeled, ends cut flat,
    and spiralized into spaghetti noodles

2 tablespoons olive oil

1 onion, sliced

12 ounces ground beef

3 garlic cloves, minced

1 (14-ounce) can of crushed tomatoes, undrained

1 cup Basic Meat or Poultry Stock (page 225),
    chicken or beef

1 teaspoon onion powder

1 teaspoon dried thyme

½ teaspoon sea salt

¼ teaspoon freshly ground black pepper

1. After spiralizing, cut the carrot noodles into elbow macaroni shapes and set aside.

2. In a large pot, heat the olive oil over medium-high heat until it shimmers.

3. Add the onion and cook, stirring frequently, until it begins to soften, about 4 minutes. Reduce the heat to medium-low and continue to cook the onion, stirring occasionally, until brown and caramelized, about 20 minutes. Remove the onion from the pan and set aside.

4. In the same pan, brown the ground beef over medium-high heat, crumbling it with a spoon, until the meat is cooked through, about 5 minutes.

5. Add the garlic and cook, stirring constantly, until it is fragrant, 30 to 60 seconds.

6. Add the crushed tomatoes and stock, scraping any browned bits from the bottom of the pan with the side of a spoon. Bring the mixture to a simmer.

7. Return the reserved onion to the pot along with the onion powder, dried thyme, salt, pepper, and carrot macaroni noodles. Cook until the noodles are al dente, 5 to 7 minutes.

CHICKEN ZOODLE SOUP

PREP TIME: 10 MINUTES / COOK TIME: 20 MINUTES

 HAND-CRANK
- Shredder blade
- Blade D

HOURGLASS
- Thin-cutting blade

SERVES 4

GLUTEN-FREE,
PALEO-FRIENDLY

PER SERVING: Calories: 376;
Total Fat: 23g; Saturated Fat: 4g;
Cholesterol: 76mg;
Total Carbs: 10g; Fiber: 2g;
Protein: 34g

Classic chicken soup gets a low-carb upgrade with the use of zucchini noodles. While the noodles offer a different texture than pasta noodles, the flavor of all of the ingredients combined is still pure deliciousness, perfect for the next time you feel a cold coming on or just have a craving for a warming, comforting soup.

4 tablespoons olive oil, divided
12 ounces skinless chicken breast,
    cut into 1-inch cubes
1 onion, chopped
1 celery stalk, chopped
1 carrot, peeled and sliced
2 garlic cloves, minced
6 cups Basic Meat or Poultry Stock (page 225),
    made from chicken
1 teaspoon dried thyme
¼ teaspoon sea salt
¼ teaspoon fresh ground black pepper
2 zucchini, ends cut flat and spiralized
    into spaghetti noodles

1. In a large pot, heat 2 tablespoons of the olive oil over medium-high heat until it shimmers.

2. Add the chicken and cook, stirring frequently, until it is cooked through, about 7 minutes. Set the chicken aside on a platter.

3. In the same pot, heat the remaining 2 tablespoons of olive oil over medium-high heat until it shimmers.

4. Add the onion, celery, and carrot and cook, stirring occasionally, until the vegetables are soft, 5 to 7 minutes.

5. Add the garlic and cook, stirring constantly, until it is fragrant, 30 to 60 seconds.

6. Add the chicken stock, scraping any browned bits from the bottom of the pan with the side of the spoon. Add the dried thyme, salt, and pepper. Bring the soup to a simmer.

7. Add the zucchini noodles and continue to cook, stirring occasionally, until the zoodles are al dente, about 5 minutes.

6

VEGETARIAN & VEGAN

LEMON–BASIL CARROT RISOTTO

PREP TIME: 10 MINUTES / COOK TIME: 10 MINUTES

 HAND-CRANK
- Shredder blade
- Blade D

HOURGLASS
- Thin-cutting blade

SERVES 4

GLUTEN-FREE,
PALEO-FRIENDLY, VEGAN

PER SERVING: Calories: 203;
Total Fat: 14g; Saturated Fat: 5g;
Cholesterol: 0mg; Total Carbs: 19g;
Fiber: 5g; Protein: 2g

Carrots make a sweet risotto in this grain-free dish. Lemon and basil make a classic flavor combination that perfectly complements the sweet, earthy flavor of the carrots. If you wish to make this dish slightly lower in carbs, you can use zucchini in place of the carrots.

8 large carrots, peeled, ends cut flat,
    and spiralized into spaghetti noodles
3 tablespoons olive oil
1 onion, finely chopped
2 garlic cloves, minced
Zest and juice of 1 lemon
¼ cup Basic Vegetable Stock (page 224)
    or store-bought
¼ cup almond milk
½ teaspoon sea salt
¼ teaspoon freshly ground black pepper
¼ cup basil leaves, cut into chiffonade

1. In a food processor, pulse the carrot noodles until they resemble rice, 10 to 20 one-second pulses. Set aside.

2. In a large sauté pan, heat the olive oil over medium-high heat until it shimmers.

3. Add the onion and cook, stirring occasionally, until the onion is soft, about 5 minutes.

4. Add the garlic and cook, stirring constantly, until it is fragrant, 30 to 60 seconds.

5. Add the lemon zest and juice, stock, almond milk, salt, pepper, and reserved carrot rice. Cook, stirring occasionally, until the carrots are al dente, about 5 minutes.

6. Stir in the basil and serve immediately.

Substitution tip: If you aren't vegan and you want a creamier risotto, just before you stir in the rice, add 2 tablespoons of unsalted butter and ¼ cup of grated Parmesan cheese. Stir until it melts, and then add the basil.

RAW CUCUMBER NOODLES
WITH ALMOND BUTTER VINAIGRETTE

PREP TIME: 10 MINUTES

HAND-CRANK
- Shredder blade
- Blade D

HOURGLASS
- Thin-cutting blade

SERVES 4

GLUTEN-FREE,
PALEO-FRIENDLY, VEGAN

PER SERVING: Calories: 356;
Total Fat: 27g; Saturated Fat: 3g;
Cholesterol: 0mg; Total Carbs: 20g;
Fiber: 3g; Protein: 12g

Creamy nut butter combines with tangy rice vinegar for an addicting vinaigrette you'll find yourself making again and again. When added to refreshing raw cucumber noodles, this dish has it all—a little sweet, a little spice, and a little crispiness. It makes a great lunch, because it travels well.

4 cucumbers, peeled, ends cut flat,
   and spiralized into spaghetti noodles
1 cup Nut Butter Sauce (page 231),
   made with almond butter
¼ cup rice vinegar
½ teaspoon stevia
½ teaspoon homemade Sriracha (page 228)
   or store-bought
¼ teaspoon sea salt
2 scallions (white and green parts), thinly sliced

1. Pat the cucumber noodles dry with a paper towel and put them in a large bowl.

2. In a small bowl, whisk together the nut butter sauce, rice vinegar, stevia, sriracha, and salt.

3. Toss the cucumber pasta with the vinaigrette. Serve garnished with the sliced scallions

Cooking tip: *If you prefer to eat the cucumber noodles cooked, you can sauté them in 2 tablespoons of olive oil, stirring occasionally, until they are al dente, 3 to 5 minutes.*

RAW ZOODLES WITH AVOCADO SAUCE

PREP TIME: 10 MINUTES

HAND-CRANK
- Shredder blade
- Blade D

HOURGLASS
- Thin-cutting blade

___

SERVES 4

___

GLUTEN-FREE,
PALEO-FRIENDLY, VEGAN

___

PER SERVING: Calories: 255;
Total Fat: 23g; Saturated Fat: 4g;
Cholesterol: 0mg; Total Carbs: 14g;
Fiber: 6g; Protein: 4g

This meal is so easy it comes together in a matter of minutes. Avocados work well with a number of flavor profiles, and they combine with zesty Southwestern flavors for a delicious sauce.

1 avocado, peeled and pitted
¼ cup olive oil
2 garlic cloves, minced
Juice of 2 limes
½ teaspoon ground cumin
1 chipotle chile in adobo sauce, minced
Dash cayenne
¼ cup chopped fresh cilantro
¼ cup vinegar
½ teaspoon sea salt
4 zucchini, ends cut flat and spiralized
    into spaghetti noodles
3 scallions (white and green parts), thinly sliced

1. In a food processor or blender, combine the avocado, olive oil, garlic, lime juice, cumin, chipotle chile, cayenne, cilantro, vinegar, and salt. Process until smooth.

2. In a large bowl, toss the sauce with the noodles. Garnish with the scallions.

Substitution tip: *These flavors also blend very well with crispy jicama, so feel free to replace the zucchini noodles with jicama. If you wish to cook your zoodles, you may do so by sautéing them in 2 tablespoons of olive oil until al dente, about 3 minutes.*

ZUCCHINI PAPPARDELLE
WITH MUSHROOMS AND TOMATO SAUCE

PREP TIME: 10 MINUTES / COOK TIME: 20 MINUTES

 IDEAL FOR HAND-CRANK
SPIRALIZERS
- Straight blade
- Blade A

SERVES 4

GLUTEN-FREE,
PALEO-FRIENDLY, VEGAN

PER SERVING: Calories: 428;
Total Fat: 25g; Saturated Fat: 3g;
Cholesterol: 0mg; Total Carbs: 45g;
Fiber: 9g; Protein: 12g

Spiralizer alternative: *If you
don't have a hand-crank
spiralizer, you can cut the
zucchini into ribbons using a
vegetable peeler.*

*Savory mushrooms take center stage in this quick and easy
meal, made with wide flat noodles to hold the sauce. This recipe
calls for a sprinkling of nutritional yeast at the end, imparting
a savory, cheesy flavor for vegans and nonvegans alike. If cheese
isn't on your no list, you can replace the nutritional yeast with
¼ cup grated Asiago.*

FOR THE PASTA

4 medium zucchini, ends cut flat
    and spiralized into ribboned noodles
Sea salt
2 tablespoons olive oil
¼ cup water

FOR THE SAUCE

2 tablespoons olive oil
1 onion, minced
16 ounces crimini mushrooms, sliced
4 garlic cloves, minced
1 (14-ounce) can crushed tomatoes, undrained
¼ teaspoon crushed red pepper flakes
½ teaspoon sea salt
¼ freshly ground black pepper
¼ cup chopped fresh flat-leaf parsley
¼ cup nutritional yeast

TO MAKE THE PASTA

1. In a colander placed over the sink, sprinkle salt over the
zucchini noodles and allow them to sit for 30 minutes to
draw out water. Quickly rinse the noodles and pat them dry
with a paper towel.

2. In a large sauté pan, heat the olive oil over medium-high heat until it shimmers.

3. Add the zucchini noodles and cook, stirring frequently, until they begin to soften, about 4 minutes.

4. Add the water and cook until the noodles are al dente, another 2 to 3 minutes.

5. Remove the noodles from the pan with tongs and drain them in a colander.

TO MAKE THE SAUCE

1. In a large sauté pan, heat the olive oil over medium-high heat until it shimmers.

2. Add the onion and mushrooms and cook, stirring occasionally, until the vegetables begin to brown, 6 to 8 minutes.

3. Add the garlic and cook, stirring constantly, until it is fragrant, 30 to 60 seconds.

4. Add the crushed tomatoes, red pepper flakes, salt, and pepper. Simmer, stirring occasionally, for 10 minutes.

5. Stir the parsley and the drained, cooked zucchini noodles into the warm sauce. Serve immediately, topped with nutritional yeast.

ROASTED SWEET POTATO PASTA
WITH KALE AND WALNUT PESTO

PREP TIME: 10 MINUTES / COOK TIME: 20 MINUTES

 IDEAL FOR HAND-CRANK
SPIRALIZERS
- Shredder blade
- Blade D

SERVES 4

GLUTEN-FREE,
PALEO-FRIENDLY,
VEGETARIAN

PER SERVING: Calories: 199;
Total Fat: 7g; Saturated Fat: 6g;
Cholesterol: 0mg; Total Carbs: 30g;
Fiber: 10g; Protein: 7g

Spiralizer alternative: *An hour-glass spiralizer will not work for the sweet potato. Instead, thinly slice the potato with a mandoline or a sharp knife.*

Roasting the sweet potato noodles gives them a nice, dry texture that holds the pesto very well. The pesto has a hint of orange in it, as well as a little bit of a spicy kick, which blends well with the earthy sweet flavors of the potatoes. If you'd like a less spicy dish, eliminate the red pepper flakes.

FOR THE SWEET POTATO PASTA
2 sweet potatoes, peeled, ends cut flat,
    and spiralized into spaghetti noodles
2 tablespoons olive oil
½ teaspoon sea salt

FOR THE PESTO
1 bunch kale, stems removed
2 garlic cloves, minced
Zest and juice of ½ orange
¼ teaspoon crushed red pepper flakes
¼ cup walnuts
¼ cup grated Parmesan cheese
    (or nutritional yeast)
¼ cup olive oil
½ teaspoon sea salt
¼ teaspoon freshly ground black pepper

1. Preheat the oven to 400°F.

2. In a large bowl, toss the potatoes with the olive oil and salt.

3. Lay in a single layer on one or two baking sheets.

4. Bake until the potatoes are al dente, 12 to 17 minutes.

TO MAKE THE PESTO

1. In the bowl of a food processor, combine the kale, garlic, orange zest and juice, red pepper flakes, walnuts, cheese, olive oil, salt, and pepper

2. Process until it forms a smooth pesto, about 1 minute.

3. Toss the pesto with the cooked noodles.

MEXICAN RICE WITH CHEESE AND AVOCADO

PREP TIME: 10 MINUTES / COOK TIME: 15 MINUTES

IDEAL FOR HAND-CRANK
SPIRALIZERS
- Shredder blade
- Blade D

SERVES 4

GLUTEN-FREE, VEGETARIAN

PER SERVING: Calories: 299;
Total Fat: 19g; Saturated Fat: 5g;
Cholesterol: 7mg; Total Carbs: 29g;
Fiber: 14g; Protein: 6g

Spiralizer alternative: *If you
have an hourglass spiralizer,
you can replace the jicama
with 2 large, peeled carrots.
Spiralize using the thin-
cutting blade.*

*Jicama makes a perfect rice base for this lime-and-cilantro-
scented Mexican dish. While the recipe calls for pepper Jack
cheese, you can choose any type of cheese you want with this
recipe. Likewise, to make this recipe vegan, leave out the cheese
altogether. While the recipe appears to be quite high in carbs
(29 grams), 14 of them are fiber, leaving each serving with 15 net
grams of carbs.*

1 medium jicama, peeled and spiralized
    into spaghetti noodles
2 tablespoons olive oil
1 onion, chopped
1 green bell pepper, chopped and seeded
1 jalapeño, seeded and minced
Juice of 2 limes
1 (14-ounce) can of tomatoes and peppers,
    such as Ro-Tel
¼ cup chopped fresh cilantro
¼ cup pepper Jack cheese
1 avocado, peeled, pitted, and sliced

1. In the bowl of a food processor, pulse the jicama noodles
until they resemble rice, 10 to 20 one-second pulses.
Set aside.

2. In a large sauté pan, heat the olive oil over medium-high
heat until it shimmers.

3. Add the onion, bell pepper, and jalapeño and cook,
stirring occasionally, until vegetables begin to brown, about
7 minutes.

4. Add the lime juice and canned tomatoes and peppers. Bring to a simmer. Add the reserved rice. Simmer until the rice is soft, 5 to 10 minutes.

5. Stir in the cilantro.

6. Stir in the cheese and cook until it melts.

7. Serve topped with avocado slices.

Substitution tip: *If you can't find Ro-Tel, you may replace it with 14 ounces of prepared salsa.*

RAW PAD THAI
WITH DAIKON RADISH AND CUCUMBER NOODLES

PREP TIME: 20 MINUTES

HAND-CRANK
- Shredder blade
- Blade D

HOURGLASS
- Thin-cutting blade

SERVES 4

GLUTEN-FREE,
PALEO-FRIENDLY, VEGAN

PER SERVING: Calories: 228;
Total Fat: 12g; Saturated Fat: 1g;
Cholesterol: 41mg;
Total Carbs: 25g; Fiber: 5g;
Protein: 9g

Pad thai is typically made with rice noodles. While the classic version is delicious, it is also extremely high in carbs. This raw version gives you lots of healthy veggies while still tasting wonderful. Daikon radish adds a light peppery taste, while the cucumbers are light and refreshing.

FOR THE PAD THAI

1 daikon radish, peeled, ends cut flat,
    and spiralized into spaghetti noodles
2 cucumbers, peeled, ends cut flat,
    and spiralized into spaghetti noodles
2 large carrots, peeled, ends cut flat,
    and spiralized into spaghetti noodles
1 cup red cabbage, shredded
4 scallions (white and green parts), thinly sliced
1 red bell pepper, seeded and thinly sliced
1 green bell pepper, seeded and chopped
1 cup bean sprouts
¼ cup chopped fresh cilantro

FOR THE SAUCE

¼ cup almond butter
2 garlic cloves, minced
Juice of 2 limes
2 tablespoons wheat-free tamari
    or coconut aminos
1 tablespoon rice vinegar
¼ teaspoon stevia
2 teaspoons sesame oil
½ teaspoon chili oil

In a large bowl, toss together the daikon radish noodles, cucumber noodles, carrot noodles, red cabbage, scallion, red and green bell peppers, bean sprouts, and cilantro.

TO MAKE THE SAUCE

1. In a small bowl, whisk together the almond butter, garlic, lime juice, tamari, rice vinegar, stevia, sesame oil, and chili oil.

2. Toss the sauce with the pad thai and serve immediately.

Cooking tip: *For cooked pad thai, sauté the radish, cucumber, carrot noodles, and cabbage in 3 tablespoons of olive oil for about 5 minutes.*

SESAME CUCUMBER NOODLES

PREP TIME: 10 MINUTES

HAND-CRANK
- Shredder blade
- Blade D

HOURGLASS
- Thin-cutting blade

SERVES 4

GLUTEN-FREE,
PALEO-FRIENDLY, VEGAN

PER SERVING: Calories: 225;
Total Fat: 18g; Saturated Fat: 3g;
Cholesterol: 0mg; Total Carbs: 14g;
Fiber: 2g; Protein: 3g

This recipe comes together with minimal effort. When combined with ginger, garlic, and vinegar, sesame oil creates a flavorful dressing that goes with refreshing cucumber noodles. If you're not on a gluten-free diet, feel free to use low-sodium soy sauce in place of the tamari or coconut aminos.

4 cucumbers, peeled, ends cut flat, and
    spiralized into spaghetti noodles
2 tablespoons sesame seeds
1 tablespoon wheat-free tamari
    or coconut aminos
3 tablespoons rice vinegar
1 teaspoon sesame oil
¼ cup olive oil
1 garlic clove, minced
½ teaspoon grated ginger
¼ teaspoon sea salt
2 scallions (white and green parts), thinly sliced

1. Pat the cucumber noodles dry with a paper towel and put them in a large bowl with the sesame seeds.

2. In a small bowl, whisk together the tamari, rice vinegar, sesame oil, olive oil, garlic, ginger, and salt.

3. Toss the sauce with the cucumber noodles. Garnish with the sliced scallions.

> **Cooking tip:** *If you prefer your cucumber noodles cooked, then sauté them in 2 tablespoons of olive oil for 3 to 5 minutes, until they are al dente.*

ZOODLE PUTTANESCA

PREP TIME: 10 MINUTES / COOK TIME: 15 MINUTES

HAND-CRANK
- Shredder blade
- Blade D

HOURGLASS
- Thin-cutting blade

SERVES 4

GLUTEN-FREE,
PALEO-FRIENDLY, VEGAN

PER SERVING: Calories: 225;
Total Fat: 10g; Saturated Fat: 2g;
Cholesterol: 0mg; Total Carbs: 30g;
Fiber: 11g; Protein: 9g

The term spaghetti alla puttanesca *(its Italian name) translates literally as "spaghetti of the whore." A southern Italian peasant dish, puttanesca sauce is nicely salty from the olives and capers. This richly flavored sauce is perfect with zoodles.*

2 tablespoons olive oil
1 onion, finely chopped
3 garlic cloves, finely minced
2 tablespoons tomato paste
½ teaspoon crushed red pepper flakes
2 (14-ounce) cans crushed tomatoes, undrained
1½ teaspoons dried oregano
2 tablespoons capers, drained
¾ cup pitted and chopped black olives
3 tablespoons chopped fresh flat-leaf parsley
4 zucchini, ends cut flat and spiralized into
    spaghetti noodles

1. In a large sauté pan, heat the olive oil over medium-high heat until it shimmers.

2. Add the onion and cook, stirring occasionally, until the onion is soft, about 5 minutes.

3. Add the garlic and cook, stirring constantly, until it is fragrant, 30 to 60 seconds.

4. Add the tomato paste and cook, stirring constantly, until it begins to brown, about 3 minutes more.

5. Add the red pepper flakes, tomatoes, oregano, capers, and olives. Simmer until mixture thickens, about 10 minutes.

6. Stir in the parsley and zoodles. Cook until the zoodles are tender, about 4 minutes.

ZUCCHINI NOODLES
WITH CREAMY MUSHROOM SAUCE

PREP TIME: 15 MINUTES / COOK TIME: 15 MINUTES

HAND-CRANK
- Chipper blade
- Blade B

HOURGLASS
- Thick-cutting blade

SERVES 4

GLUTEN-FREE, VEGETARIAN

PER SERVING: Calories: 246;
Total Fat: 19g; Saturated Fat: 8g;
Cholesterol: 26mg;
Total Carbs: 13g; Fiber: 3g;
Protein: 6g

This simple mushroom cream sauce works with zucchini fettuc-cine perfectly. The wider noodles hold up well to the heaviness of the sauce. To avoid watering down the sauce, salt the zucchini noodles and allow them to drain in a colander for 30 minutes before cooking them.

FOR THE NOODLES

4 zucchini, peeled, ends cut flat, and
    spiralized into fettuccine noodles

Salt

2 tablespoons olive oil

FOR THE SAUCE

2 tablespoons butter

2 tablespoons minced shallot

12 ounces crimini mushrooms, sliced

2 garlic cloves, minced

¼ cup dry white wine

1 cup Basic Vegetable Stock (page 224)
    or store-bought

1 teaspoon chopped fresh thyme

½ teaspoon sea salt

¼ freshly ground black pepper

Pinch crushed red pepper flakes

½ cup heavy cream

2 tablespoons chopped fresh flat-leaf parsley

TO MAKE THE NOODLES

1. In a colander placed over the sink, generously salt the zucchini noodles and allow them to sit for 30 minutes to drain excess water. Quickly rinse the noodles and pat them dry with the paper towels.

2. In a large sauté pan, heat the olive oil over medium-high heat until it shimmers. Add the dried noodles and cook, stirring occasionally, until they are al dente, about 5 minutes.

TO MAKE THE SAUCE

1. In a large sauté pan, melt the butter over medium-high heat. Add the shallots and mushrooms and cook, stirring occasionally, until the mushrooms brown, about 7 minutes.

2. Add the garlic and cook, stirring constantly, until fragrant, 30 to 60 seconds.

3. Add the wine and simmer for 2 minutes.

4. Add the vegetable stock, thyme, salt, pepper, and red pepper flakes. Simmer for 5 minutes.

5. Stir in the heavy cream and cook for 1 to 2 minutes to heat through, stirring constantly.

6. Stir in the parsley.

7. Toss with the noodles and serve.

Cooking tip: *Mushrooms are like little sponges that will soak up water, so you shouldn't clean them by rinsing. Instead, use a mushroom brush or paper towel to wipe away any dirt.*

SWEET POTATO FETTUCCINE
WITH BROCCOLINI AND ROASTED GARLIC

PREP TIME: 15 MINUTES / COOK TIME: 30 MINUTES

IDEAL FOR HAND-CRANK
SPIRALIZERS

- Chipper blade
- Blade B

SERVES 4

GLUTEN-FREE, VEGETARIAN

PER SERVING: Calories: 636;
Total Fat: 47g; Saturated Fat: 30g;
Cholesterol: 139mg;
Total Carbs: 43g; Fiber: 6g;
Protein: 13g

Spiralizer alternative: *An hour-glass spiralizer will not work with a sweet potato. Instead, use a vegetable peeler to shave the sweet potato into thin strips, and cut the strips into fettuccine-shaped noodles.*

The only words to describe this dish are "pure decadence." While it's not an everyday meal, it's definitely a delicious occasional treat. The rich cream sauce in this fettuccine is very filling, so a little bit goes a long way. Many grocery stores sell roasted garlic in the deli section, so if you can find it, that will save you time in the kitchen. If not, cut the top off a bulb of garlic, drizzle it with olive oil, and bake it wrapped in foil in a 350° oven for about an hour. To use the garlic, squeeze it from the papery skins.

¼ cup plus 4 tablespoons unsalted butter, divided

3 sweet potatoes, peeled, ends cut flat,
    cut into fettuccine noodles

1 onion, chopped

2 cups broccolini

8 cloves of roasted garlic, sliced

¼ teaspoon crushed red pepper flakes

8 ounces cream cheese, cubed

¼ cup heavy cream

¼ cup grated Parmesan cheese

½ teaspoon sea salt

¼ teaspoon freshly ground black pepper

1. Preheat the oven to 400°F.

2. In a skillet or saucepan melt 2 tablespoons of the butter. In a large bowl, toss the sweet potato noodles with the butter.

3. Spread the noodles on one or two cookie sheets and bake them in the preheated oven until they are al dente, about 17 minutes.

4. In a large sauté pan, heat 2 tablespoons of the butter over medium-high heat.

5. Add the onion and broccolini and cook, stirring occasionally, until the broccolini is soft, about 7 minutes.

6. Add the garlic and red pepper flakes and continue to cook, stirring constantly, for 1 minute.

7. While the broccolini and potato noodles cook, in a large saucepan over medium heat, combine the remaining ¼ cup butter, cream cheese, heavy cream, Parmesan cheese, salt, and pepper.

8. Cook, stirring constantly, until the sauce is combined and the cheeses are melted together, about 4 minutes.

9. In a large bowl, toss the sauce, broccolini mixture, and noodles together.

SWEET POTATO CAKES
WITH ORANGE–SRIRACHA AIOLI

PREP TIME: 15 MINUTES / COOK TIME: 30 MINUTES

 IDEAL FOR HAND-CRANK
SPIRALIZERS
- Shredder blade
- Blade D

SERVES 4

GLUTEN-FREE,
PALEO-FRIENDLY,
VEGETARIAN

PER SERVING: Calories: 485;
Total Fat: 29g; Saturated Fat: 25g;
Cholesterol: 0mg; Total Carbs: 55g;
Fiber: 10g; Protein: 6g

Spiralizer alternative: *If you
have an hourglass spiralizer,
you can substitute 6 large carrots for the sweet potatoes.*

*Baked sweet potato cakes are crispy on the outside and tender
on the inside. The orange-sriracha aioli adds a lot of zip to these
tasty cakes. The sweet potato cakes, once cooled, also make a
fantastic bread for sandwiches and burgers.*

FOR THE SWEET POTATO CAKES

2 sweet potatoes, peeled, ends cut flat,
   and spiralized into spaghetti noodles

¼ cup coconut oil, melted

1 egg, beaten

½ teaspoon homemade Sriracha (page 228)
   or store-bought

½ onion, chopped

2 garlic cloves, minced

½ cup almond meal

½ teaspoon sea salt

¼ teaspoon freshly ground black pepper

FOR THE AIOLI

1 cup Garlic Aioli (page 229)

1 teaspoon homemade Sriracha (page 228)
   or store-bought

Zest of 1 orange

1. Preheat the oven to 375°F.

2. Line a baking sheet with parchment paper.

3. Cut the sweet potato noodles into 2-inch pieces.

4. In a large bowl, whisk together the coconut oil, egg, and sriracha. Stir in the sweet potato noodles, onion, garlic, almond meal, salt, and pepper.

5. Spoon the mixture onto the prepared baking sheet in eight equal parts.

6. Bake in the preheated oven for 15 minutes. Flip with a spatula and bake for an additional 15 minutes, until cooked through and golden.

7. Serve topped with the aioli or cool and use as sandwich bread.

TO MAKE THE AIOLI

1. In a small bowl, whisk together the garlic aioli, sriracha, and orange zest.

2. Serve on top of the sweet potato cakes.

CUCUMBER NOODLES
WITH GARLIC, LEMON, CASHEWS, AND CUMIN

PREP TIME: 10 MINUTES / COOK TIME: 15 MINUTES

HAND-CRANK
- Shredder blade
- Blade D

HOURGLASS
- Thin-cutting blade

SERVES 4

GLUTEN-FREE, VEGAN

PER SERVING: Calories: 193;
Total Fat: 12g; Saturated Fat: 2g;
Cholesterol: 0mg; Total Carbs: 20g;
Fiber: 3g; Protein: 5g

If you prefer your veggies raw, you don't need to cook these noodles even though the recipe calls for it. Cumin and garlic add warm flavors to the dish, while lemon adds a bright acidity that balances those spices. The cashews add a tasty crunch.

4 cucumbers, peeled, ends cut flat,
    and spiralized into spaghetti noodles
2 tablespoons olive oil
1 onion, finely chopped
1 red bell pepper, chopped and seeded
3 garlic cloves, finely chopped
Zest of 1 lemon, plus juice of 2 lemons
1 cup Basic Vegetable Stock (page 224)
1 teaspoon ground cumin
½ teaspoon sea salt
¼ teaspoon freshly ground black pepper
¼ cup chopped cashews

1. Pat the cucumber noodles dry with a paper towel.

2. In a large sauté pan, heat the olive oil over medium-high heat until it shimmers.

3. Add the onion and bell pepper and cook, stirring occasionally, until the onion is soft, about 5 minutes.

4. Add the garlic and cook, stirring constantly, until it is fragrant, 30 to 60 seconds.

5. Add the lemon zest and juice, stock, cumin, salt, and pepper. Bring to a simmer.

6. Add the cucumber noodles and cook, stirring occasionally, until the noodles are soft, about 2 minutes. Toss with the cashews and serve.

AVOCADO AND TOMATO SANDWICHES
ON CARROT–PARMESAN BUNS

PREP TIME: 15 MINUTES / COOK TIME: 30 MINUTES

HAND-CRANK
- Shredder blade
- Blade D

HOURGLASS
- Thin-cutting blade

SERVES 4

GLUTEN-FREE, VEGETARIAN

PER SERVING: Calories: 397;
Total Fat: 32g; Saturated Fat: 16g;
Cholesterol: 46mg;
Total Carbs: 23g; Fiber: 9g;
Protein: 9g

The carrot-Parmesan buns are a variation of the Sweet Potato Cakes found earlier in this chapter (page 116). Grated Parmesan cheese adds a savory bite to the buns.

FOR THE BUNS

6 large carrots, peeled, ends cut flat,
    and spiralized into spaghetti noodles

¼ cup olive oil

1 egg, beaten

½ onion, finely chopped

2 garlic cloves, minced

½ cup almond meal

½ cup grated Parmesan cheese

½ teaspoon sea salt

¼ teaspoon freshly ground black pepper

FOR THE SANDWICH

1 avocado, pitted and peeled

1 tablespoon freshly squeezed lemon juice

2 heirloom tomatoes, thickly sliced

TO MAKE THE BUNS

1. Preheat the oven to 375°F.

2. Line a baking sheet with parchment paper.

3. Cut the carrot noodles into 2-inch pieces.

4. In a large bowl, whisk together the olive oil and egg. Stir in the carrot noodles, onion, garlic, almond meal, Parmesan, salt, and pepper.

5. Spoon the mixture onto the prepared baking sheets in eight equal parts.

6. Bake in the preheated oven for 15 minutes. Flip with a spatula and bake for an additional 15 minutes, until cooked through and golden.

7. Allow to cool thoroughly on a wire rack.

TO MAKE THE SANDWICHES

1. In a small bowl, mash together the avocado and lemon juice with a fork.

2. Carefully spread the avocado mixture evenly on four of the buns.

3. Top with slices of heirloom tomatoes, and then top with a second bun.

> **Cooking tip:** *For a zestier sandwich, spread one side of the bread with the Garlic Aioli (page 229).*

GINGER BROCCOLI STIR-FRY
WITH SWEET POTATO NOODLES

PREP TIME: 10 MINUTES / COOK TIME: 25 MINUTES

IDEAL FOR HAND-CRANK
SPIRALIZERS

- Shredder blade
- Blade D

SERVES 4

GLUTEN-FREE,
PALEO-FRIENDLY, VEGAN

PER SERVING: Calories: 294;
Total Fat: 14g; Saturated Fat: 7g;
Cholesterol: 0mg; Total Carbs: 39g;
Fiber: 7g; Protein: 4g

Spiralizer alternative: *If you
have an hourglass spiralizer,
you can substitute 6 large carrots for the sweet potatoes.*

*Cook the noodles and the stir-fry separately in this recipe.
Then use the stir-fry like a sauce on the noodles. The ginger in
the stir-fry sauce goes beautifully with the sweet potatoes. If
you'd like fewer carbs, you can replace the sweet potatoes with
zucchini.*

FOR THE NOODLES

2 tablespoons olive oil

2 sweet potatoes, peeled, ends cut flat,
    and spiralized into spaghetti noodles

FOR THE STIR-FRY

2 tablespoons coconut oil

6 scallions (white and green parts), sliced

1 teaspoon grated ginger

2 cups broccoli florets

4 ounces shiitake mushrooms, sliced

1 red bell pepper, sliced

2 garlic cloves, finely minced

2 tablespoons wheat-free tamari
    or coconut aminos

2 tablespoons rice vinegar

1 tablespoon arrowroot powder

2 tablespoons water

¼ teaspoon crushed red pepper flakes

1. Preheat the oven to 400°F.

2. In a large bowl, toss the olive oil with the sweet potato noodles. Spread the noodles on a large baking sheet.

3. Roast in the oven until the noodles are al dente, about 17 minutes.

TO MAKE THE STIR-FRY

1. In a large sauté pan, heat the coconut oil over medium-high heat.

2. Add the scallions, ginger, broccoli, mushrooms, and red bell pepper.

3. Cook, stirring frequently, until the veggies are crisp-tender, about 4 minutes.

4. Add the garlic and cook, stirring constantly, until it is fragrant, 30 to 60 seconds.

5. Add the tamari and rice vinegar. Simmer for 2 to 3 minutes.

6. In a small bowl, whisk together the arrowroot powder, water, and red pepper flakes. Add them to the stir-fry. Cook until the sauce thickens slightly, about 1 minute.

7. Serve the stir-fry over the sweet potato noodles.

7

FISH & SEAFOOD

CARROT PAELLA

PREP TIME: 10 MINUTES / COOK TIME: 20 MINUTES

HAND-CRANK

- Shredder blade
- Blade D

HOURGLASS

- Thin-cutting blade

SERVES 4

GLUTEN-FREE,
PALEO-FRIENDLY

PER SERVING: Calories: 337;
Total Fat: 24g; Saturated Fat: 7g;
Cholesterol: 114mg;
Total Carbs: 14g; Fiber: 3g;
Protein: 18g

Valencia, which sits on the coast of Spain, has served some form of paella for centuries. It's a saffron-scented rice dish with vegetables and a mix of meat, fish, and poultry. Here, seafood takes center stage. The sweet earthiness of the carrots mixes well with the sweet flesh of the shellfish. The chorizo adds a nice spiciness to the dish.

6 carrots, peeled, ends cut flat, and spiralized
  into spaghetti noodles
2 tablespoons olive oil
6 ounces chorizo
1 onion, chopped
3 garlic cloves, minced
6 ounces medium shrimp, peeled and deveined
1 cup Basic Meat or Poultry Stock (page 225),
  made with chicken
Pinch saffron
½ teaspoon sea salt
¼ teaspoon freshly ground black pepper
3 tablespoons chopped fresh flat-leaf parsley

1. In the bowl of a food processor, pulse the carrot noodles until it resembles rice, 10 to 15 one-second pulses. Set aside.

2. In a large sauté pan, heat the olive oil over medium-high heat until it shimmers.

3. Add the chorizo and cook, stirring frequently, until it is browned, about 5 minutes. Remove the chorizo from the fat with a slotted spoon and set it aside on a platter.

4. Add the onion and cook, stirring occasionally, until it is soft, about 5 minutes.

5. Add the garlic and cook, stirring constantly, until it is fragrant, 30 to 60 seconds.

6. Add the reserved carrot rice, reserved chorizo, shrimp, chicken stock, saffron, salt, and pepper. Cook, stirring frequently, until the carrot rice is cooked and the shrimp is pink, about 5 minutes.

7. Remove from the heat. Stir in the parsley. Serve immediately.

Cooking tip: *To prepare the shrimp, remove the peel and the tail. Using a sharp knife, slit along the curve on the back of the shrimp and remove the vein.*

PAN-SEARED SEA SCALLOPS
ON MUSHROOM–ZUCCHINI RICE

PREP TIME: 10 MINUTES / COOK TIME: 20 MINUTES

HAND-CRANK
- Shredder blade
- Blade D

HOURGLASS
- Thin-cutting blade

SERVES 4

GLUTEN-FREE

PER SERVING: Calories: 362;
Total Fat: 16g; Saturated Fat: 2g;
Cholesterol: 37mg;
Total Carbs: 22g; Fiber: 8g;
Protein: 30g

Begin your prep for this dish in the morning before you head to work. Pour the chicken stock over the dried porcini mushrooms to allow them to infuse the broth. The earthiness of the mushroom-infused broth makes a great sauce for the sweet sea scallops.

3 ounces dried porcini mushrooms

2 cups Basic Meat or Poultry Stock (page 225),
    made with chicken, heated to simmering

3 zucchini, ends cut flat and spiralized into
    spaghetti noodles

1 pound sea scallops

1 teaspoon sea salt, divided

½ teaspoon freshly ground black pepper, divided

4 tablespoons olive oil, divided

½ onion, finely chopped

6 ounces button mushrooms, sliced

3 garlic cloves, minced

1 teaspoon chopped fresh thyme

1. In a medium-sized heatproof bowl, pour the hot stock over the mushrooms. Cover, refrigerate, and allow to steep for at least three hours.

2. Remove the mushrooms from the broth and roughly chop them. Set the mushrooms and the broth aside.

3. In the bowl of a food processor fitted with a chopping blade, process the zucchini noodles until it resembles rice, about 10 one-second pulses. Set aside.

4. Season the scallops with ½ teaspoon of the salt and ¼ teaspoon of the pepper.

5. In a large sauté pan over medium-high heat, heat 2 tablespoons of the olive oil until it shimmers.

6. Add the scallops and cook without moving until they are opaque, about 3 minutes per side.

7. Remove the scallops from the oil with tongs and set them aside on a platter, tented with foil to keep them warm.

8. Add the remaining 2 tablespoons of olive oil to the pan. Add the onion, button mushrooms, and reserved chopped porcini mushrooms. Cook, stirring occasionally, until the vegetables begin to brown, about 6 minutes.

9. Add the garlic and cook, stirring constantly, until it is fragrant, 30 to 60 seconds.

10. Add the reserved chicken stock, reserved zucchini rice, remaining ½ teaspoon salt, remaining ¼ teaspoon pepper, and thyme. Cook, stirring occasionally, until the rice is soft, about 5 minutes.

11. Serve the rice topped with the scallops.

Cooking tip: *Sea scallops often have a large tendon on the side that needs to be removed because it becomes remarkably tough when cooked. Use a sharp knife to carefully pull the tendon away from the scallop.*

SHRIMP FRA DIAVOLO
ON ZUCCHINI SPAGHETTI

PREP TIME: 10 MINUTES / COOK TIME: 30 MINUTES

 HAND-CRANK
- Shredder blade
- Blade D

HOURGLASS
- Thin-cutting blade

SERVES 4

GLUTEN-FREE,
PALEO-FRIENDLY

PER SERVING: Calories: 433;
Total Fat: 25g; Saturated Fat: 4g;
Cholesterol: 162mg;
Total Carbs: 21g; Fiber: 5g;
Protein: 26g

Fra diavolo in Italian means "brother devil." When you see this term in recipes, get ready for some heat, because anything labeled fra diavolo is usually pretty fiery. This tasty shrimp dish is no exception. It gets its heat from a heaping helping of crushed red pepper flakes.

FOR THE NOODLES

3 tablespoons olive oil

6 zucchini, ends cut flat and spiralized
   into spaghetti noodles

FOR THE SHRIMP

1 pound large shrimp, peeled and deveined

1 teaspoon crushed red pepper flakes

½ teaspoon sea salt

4 tablespoons olive oil, divided

1 onion, chopped

3 garlic cloves

1 cup dry white wine

1 (14-ounce) can diced tomatoes, undrained

½ teaspoon oregano

¼ teaspoon freshly ground black pepper

3 tablespoons chopped fresh flat-leaf parsley

TO MAKE THE NOODLES

1. In a large sauté pan, heat the olive oil over medium-high heat until it shimmers.

2. Add the zucchini noodles and cook, stirring frequently, until they are al dente, about 5 minutes.

1. In a large bowl, combine the shrimp, red pepper flakes, and salt. Allow them to sit for 10 minutes.

2. In a large sauté pan, heat 2 tablespoons of the olive oil over medium-high heat until it shimmers.

3. Add the shrimp and cook, stirring frequently, until it is pink, about 4 minutes. Remove the shrimp from the oil with a slotted spoon and set it aside on a platter tented with foil.

4. Add the remaining 2 tablespoons of olive oil to the sauté pan. Add the onion and cook, stirring frequently, until it is soft, about 5 minutes.

5. Add the garlic and cook, stirring constantly, until it is fragrant, 30 to 60 seconds.

6. Add the white wine and cook, scraping any browned bits from the bottom of the pan with the side of the spoon, for 3 minutes.

7. Add the tomatoes, oregano, and pepper. Cook, stirring occasionally, until the liquid from the tomatoes has evaporated slightly, about 5 minutes.

8. Add the shrimp and parsley. Cook to heat through.

9. Add the zucchini noodles and stir until coated with the sauce.

THAI HALIBUT
WITH COCONUT CURRY AND CUCUMBER NOODLES

PREP TIME: 10 MINUTES / COOK TIME: 20 MINUTES

HAND-CRANK

- Shredder blade
- Blade D

HOURGLASS

- Thin-cutting blade

SERVES 4

GLUTEN-FREE,
PALEO-FRIENDLY

PER SERVING: Calories: 414;
Total Fat: 26g; Saturated Fat: 9g;
Cholesterol: 62mg;
Total Carbs: 20g; Fiber: 3g;
Protein: 30g

A rich coconut broth infused with curry spices atop a bed of cucumber noodles serves as the base for a flaky, sweet, spiced halibut. This meal is rich, but it has a balanced acidity and sweetness that keeps it from being heavy.

FOR THE NOODLES

3 tablespoons olive oil

6 cucumbers, ends cut flat and spiralized
   into spaghetti noodles

FOR THE BROTH AND FISH

2 tablespoons olive oil

½ onion, finely chopped

2 teaspoons curry powder

2 cups Basic Meat or Poultry Stock (page 225),
   made with chicken

½ cup coconut milk

½ teaspoon salt

4 (4-ounce) halibut fillets, skin removed

¼ cup fresh chopped cilantro

2 tablespoons lime juice

TO MAKE THE NOODLES

1. In a large sauté pan, heat the olive oil over medium-high heat until it shimmers.

2. Add the cucumber noodles and cook, stirring occasionally, until al dente, about 5 minutes.

1. In a large pot, heat the olive oil over medium-high heat until it shimmers.

2. Add the onion and curry powder and cook, stirring occasionally, until the onion is soft, about 5 minutes.

3. Add the chicken stock, coconut milk, and salt. Bring to a simmer.

4. Add the halibut and coat it with sauce. Cover and cook until the halibut is flaky, about 6 minutes.

5. Remove the halibut from the broth and set it aside, tented with foil to keep warm.

6. Stir in the cilantro and lime juice.

7. In four bowls, portion the cucumber noodles. Pour the broth over the top, and finish each with a piece of the halibut.

Cooking tip: *When shopping for halibut, choose fish that doesn't have a fishy smell, which indicates freshness. The flesh should be a pearly white color.*

JAMBALAYA WITH JICAMA RICE

PREP TIME: 10 MINUTES / COOK TIME: 20 MINUTES

 IDEAL FOR HAND-CRANK
SPIRALIZERS

- Shredder blade
- Blade D

SERVES 4

GLUTEN-FREE,
PALEO-FRIENDLY

PER SERVING: Calories: 485;
Total Fat: 27g; Saturated Fat: 7g;
Cholesterol: 144mg;
Total Carbs: 32g; Fiber: 14g;
Protein: 29g

Spiralizer alternative: *If you
have an hourglass spiralizer,
you can replace the jicama with
3 large, peeled carrots.*

A Creole dish from Louisiana, jambalaya is a super spicy version of paella. It uses Andouille sausage, which has a lot of heat, as well as shrimp and, in this case, jicama rice. Traditional jambalaya takes a while to cook, but with jicama rice it's quick and easy.

1 medium jicama, peeled, ends cut flat, and
    spiralized into spaghetti noodles
3 tablespoons olive oil
8 ounces Andouille sausage, cut into
    1-inch chunks
1 onion, chopped
1 red bell pepper, seeded and chopped
1 green bell pepper, seeded and chopped
2 garlic cloves, minced
1 (14-ounce) can crushed tomatoes
1 cup Basic Meat or Poultry Stock (page 225),
    chicken or beef
1 teaspoon dried oregano
½ teaspoon sea salt
¼ teaspoon freshly ground black pepper
8 ounces medium shrimp, peeled and deveined
¼ cup chopped fresh flat-leaf parsley

1. In the bowl of a food processor fitted with a chopping blade, process the jicama noodles until it resembles rice, 10 to 20 one-second pulses. Set aside.

2. In a large pot, heat the olive oil over medium-high heat until it shimmers.

3. Add the Andouille sausage and cook, stirring occasionally, until it browns, about 5 minutes. Remove the sausage from the pot with a slotted spoon and set aside on a plate.

4. Add the onion and bell peppers and cook, stirring occasionally, until the vegetables are soft, about 5 minutes.

5. Add the garlic and cook, stirring constantly, until it is fragrant, 30 to 60 seconds.

6. Add the tomatoes, stock, oregano, salt, pepper, shrimp, reserved rice, and reserved Andouille. Cook, stirring occasionally, until the shrimp is pink, about 5 minutes.

7. Stir in the parsley, and serve.

SALMON WITH LEMON–DILL ZUCCHINI NOODLES

PREP TIME: 10 MINUTES / COOK TIME: 15 MINUTES

 HAND-CRANK
- Shredder blade
- Blade D

HOURGLASS
- Thin-cutting blade

SERVES 4

GLUTEN-FREE,
PALEO-FRIENDLY

PER SERVING: Calories: 352;
Total Fat: 25g; Saturated Fat: 4g;
Cholesterol: 50mg;
Total Carbs: 11g; Fiber: 3g;
Protein: 26g

Choose wild-caught salmon for this recipe. It has the best flavor, and it offers great nutrition including omega-3 fatty acids. The lemon and dill in the zucchini noodles are the perfect complement to the delicate flesh of the salmon.

FOR THE SALMON

4 (4-ounce) salmon fillets

½ teaspoon sea salt

¼ teaspoon freshly ground black pepper

2 tablespoons olive oil

FOR THE NOODLES

3 tablespoons olive oil

6 zucchini, ends cut flat and spiralized
  into spaghetti noodles

Zest and juice of 1 lemon

½ teaspoon sea salt

¼ teaspoon freshly ground black pepper

1 teaspoon chopped fresh dill

TO MAKE THE SALMON

1. Season the salmon with the salt and pepper.

2. In a large sauté pan, heat the olive oil over medium-high heat until it shimmers. Add the salmon, skin side down.

3. Cook, shaking the pan to keep the salmon from sticking, 3 minutes.

4. Reduce the heat and cover the pan. Continue to cook the salmon for another 3 to 5 minutes, until the flesh is opaque.

1. In a large sauté pan, heat the olive oil over medium-high heat until it shimmers. Add the zucchini and cook, stirring occasionally, 3 minutes.

2. Add the lemon zest and juice, salt, and pepper. Cook, stirring occasionally, until the noodles are al dente, about 3 minutes.

3. Stir in the dill.

4. Serve the noodles topped with the salmon fillets.

CRAB CAKES
WITH LEMON–LIME AIOLI

PREP TIME: 15 MINUTES / COOK TIME: 15 MINUTES

 HAND-CRANK
- Shredder blade
- Blade D

HOURGLASS
- Thin-cutting blade

SERVES 4

GLUTEN-FREE,
PALEO-FRIENDLY

PER SERVING: Calories: 268;
Total Fat: 25g; Saturated Fat: 2g;
Cholesterol: 66mg;
Total Carbs: 11g; Fiber: 3g;
Protein: 20g

In most crab cake recipes, bread crumbs keep the cakes light. Here, low-carb almond meal replaces the bread crumbs. Spiralized carrots cut into julienne add the perfect crunch and flavor.

FOR THE CRAB CAKES

2 carrots, peeled, ends cut flat,
    and spiralized into spaghetti noodles

1 pound lump crab meat

2½ tablespoons Garlic Aioli (page 229)

½ red bell pepper, seeded and minced

3 scallions (white and green parts), minced

½ cup almond meal

1 teaspoon Old Bay seasoning

2 tablespoons olive oil

FOR THE AIOLI

1 cup Garlic Aioli (page 229)

Zest of 1 lemon

Zest of 1 lime

1. Cut the carrot noodles into 1-inch julienne.

2. In a large bowl, combine the carrot noodles, crab, aioli, red pepper, scallions, almond meal, and Old Bay seasoning. Mix carefully to combine well. Form the mixture into eight cakes. Refrigerate for 1 hour.

3. In a large sauté pan, heat the olive oil over medium-high heat until it shimmers. Add the crab cakes and cook until golden brown on both sides, 3 to 5 minutes per side.

4. In a small bowl, mix the aioli with the lemon zest and lime zest. Serve with the crab cakes.

SMOKED SALMON
WITH CARROT SPAGHETTI

PREP TIME: 15 MINUTES / COOK TIME: 20 MINUTES

 HAND-CRANK
- Shredder blade
- Blade D

HOURGLASS
- Thin-cutting blade

SERVES 4

GLUTEN-FREE,
PALEO-FRIENDLY

PER SERVING: Calories: 269;
Total Fat: 14g; Saturated Fat: 10g;
Cholesterol: 20mg;
Total Carbs: 19g; Fiber: 4g;
Protein: 18g

This recipe has a sublime balance of flavors: sweet, smoky, and just a little bit spicy. Served atop a bed of carrot spaghetti, the sauce brings out the earthy sweetness of the carrots. It's also full of vitamin A, vitamin C, and healthy omega-3 fatty acids.

3 tablespoons coconut oil

4 scallions (white and green parts), minced

1 red bell pepper, seeded and minced

4 garlic cloves, minced

Zest and juice of 1 orange

2 tablespoons wheat-free tamari or
    coconut aminos

½ teaspoon stevia

½ teaspoon homemade Sriracha (page 228)
    or store-bought

8 carrots, peeled, ends cut flat, and spiralized
    into spaghetti noodles

12 ounces smoked salmon, chopped

1. In a large sauté pan, heat the coconut oil over medium-high heat.

2. Add the scallions and bell pepper and cook, stirring occasionally, until vegetables are soft, about 5 minutes.

3. Add the garlic and cook, stirring constantly, until it is fragrant, 30 to 60 seconds.

4. Add the orange zest and juice, tamari, stevia, sriracha, and carrot spaghetti. Cook, stirring occasionally, until the spaghetti is al dente, about 5 minutes.

5. Stir in the salmon. Cook to heat through.

8

MEAT
& POULTRY

SHEPHERD'S PIE

PREP TIME: 10 MINUTES / COOK TIME: 30 MINUTES

IDEAL FOR HAND-CRANK
SPIRALIZERS

- Straight blade
- Blade A

SERVES 4

GLUTEN-FREE

PER SERVING: Calories: 418;
Total Fat: 26g; Saturated Fat: 1g;
Cholesterol: 135mg;
Total Carbs: 11g; Fiber: 2g;
Protein: 36g

Spiralizer alternative: *If your
spiralizer doesn't come with a
pin to create slices for potatoes with the straight blade,
cut the spirals into individu-
alized rounds. An hourglass
spiralizer will not work for the
sweet potato. Instead, use a
vegetable peeler to shave it
into slices.*

*The earliest versions of shepherd's pie, also known as cottage
pie, served as a way to use leftover meat and vegetables in a new
dish. Often the day after a roast dinner, all of the elements of the
meal would show up on the table as a lovely cottage pie. Typical
shepherd's pie uses mashed potatoes. This one uses spiralized
sweet potatoes, instead.*

2 tablespoons olive oil
1 pound ground beef
1 onion, chopped
1 carrot, peeled and chopped
1 celery stalk, chopped
1 teaspoon chopped fresh thyme
½ teaspoon chopped fresh rosemary
2 tablespoons Worcestershire sauce
½ teaspoon sea salt
¼ teaspoon freshly ground black pepper
¼ cup heavy cream
1 sweet potato, peeled, ends cut flat, and
    spiralized into potato-shaped noodles
3 tablespoons butter, melted

1. Preheat the oven to 400°F.

2. In a large sauté pan, heat the olive oil over medium-high
heat until it shimmers. Add the ground beef and cook, crumbling with a spoon, until it is browned, about 5 minutes.

3. Add the onion, carrot, and celery and cook, stirring occasionally, until the vegetables are soft, about 5 minutes more.

4. Add the thyme, rosemary, Worcestershire sauce, salt,
pepper, and heavy cream. Stir to combine.

5. Put the mixture in a 9-by-9-inch baking pan.

6. Place the sweet potato rounds in an even layer over the top. Brush with the butter.

7. Bake in the preheated oven for 20 minutes, until the potatoes are golden.

Substitution tip: *Love cheese? Sprinkle 2 ounces of grated cheese over the top of the potatoes before baking.*

BEEF STROGANOFF
WITH SUMMER SQUASH NOODLES

PREP TIME: 3 HOURS SOAKING TIME, PLUS 10 MINUTES ACTIVE PREP / COOK TIME: 25 MINUTES

HAND-CRANK
- Straight blade
- Blade A

HOURGLASS
- Thick-cutting blade

SERVES 4

GLUTEN-FREE

PER SERVING: Calories: 606;
Total Fat: 26g; Saturated Fat: 14g;
Cholesterol: 146mg;
Total Carbs: 27g; Fiber: 10g;
Protein: 49g

Beef stroganoff originated in 19th century Russia. Typically made with strips of steak and mushrooms, this version uses ground beef. Choose ground beef that is 85 percent lean for best results. Use yellow summer squash (the kind that looks like yellow zucchini) for this recipe.

FOR THE NOODLES

3 tablespoons butter

6 yellow squash, ends cut flat and spiralized
    into ribboned noodles

FOR THE STROGANOFF

3 ounces dried porcini mushrooms

2 cups Basic Meat or Poultry Stock (page 225),
    made from beef

1 pound ground beef

2 tablespoons butter

1 onion, chopped

8 ounces crimini mushrooms, quartered

3 garlic cloves, minced

½ cup dry white wine

1 teaspoon dried thyme

½ teaspoon sea salt

¼ teaspoon freshly ground black pepper

¼ cup arrowroot powder

2 tablespoons Worcestershire sauce

¼ cup sour cream

¼ cup chopped fresh parsley

In a large sauté pan, heat the butter over medium-high heat. Add the noodles and cook, stirring occasionally, until al dente, about 5 minutes.

TO MAKE THE STROGANOFF

1. Soak the porcini mushrooms in the beef stock for 3 hours before cooking.

2. Remove the mushrooms from the stock and chop. Set both the mushrooms and the stock aside.

3. In a large sauté pan, brown the ground beef, crumbling with a spoon, until cooked, about 5 minutes. Remove from the pan and set aside.

4. Add the butter to the pan and cook until it is foamy. Add the onion, crimini mushrooms, and porcini mushrooms and cook, stirring occasionally, until the vegetables are browned, about 7 minutes.

5. Add the garlic and cook, stirring constantly, until it is fragrant, 30 to 60 seconds.

6. Add the white wine, scraping any browned bits from the bottom of the pan with the side of your spoon.

7. Return the ground beef to the pan, along with the thyme, salt, and pepper.

8. In a small bowl, whisk together ½ cup of the reserved stock with the arrowroot powder. Set aside.

CONTINUED

9. Add the remaining 1½ cups of stock and Worcestershire sauce to the pan. Stir in the stock and arrowroot mixture. Cook, stirring constantly, until it thickens, about 2 minutes.

10. Stir in the sour cream and parsley. Cook, stirring constantly, to heat through, 2 to 3 minutes more.

11. Serve on top of the hot noodles.

Cooking tip: *This recipe calls for you to reconstitute the dried mushrooms at least 3 hours before, but you can do it overnight or as long as 24 hours ahead of time.*

SWEDISH MEATBALLS
ON ZUCCHINI EGG NOODLES

PREP TIME: 20 MINUTES / COOK TIME: 8 HOURS

 IDEAL FOR HAND-CRANK
SPIRALIZERS

- Straight blade
- Blade A

SERVES 4

GLUTEN-FREE

PER SERVING: Calories: 648;
Total Fat: 46g Saturated Fat: 10g;
Cholesterol: 207mg;
Total Carbs: 23g; Fiber: 5g;
Protein: 40g

Spiralizer alternative: *If you
have an hourglass-shaped spiralizer, you can make linguine
zoodles using the thick-cutting
blade. The noodles won't be as
flat as you can get with a hand-
crank spiralizer, but they'll do
the job.*

*Typically, you make meatballs with a panade, which is a mix-
ture of milk and bread. This keeps the meatballs moist and gives
them their classic texture. In this recipe, almond-meal flour
stands in for the panade, keeping the meatballs light.*

FOR THE MEATBALLS

6 tablespoons olive oil, divided

1 onion, finely chopped

1 garlic clove, minced

½ pound ground beef

½ pound ground pork

¼ cup almond meal

2 egg yolks

½ teaspoon dried thyme

½ freshly ground black pepper

½ teaspoon sea salt

¼ teaspoon allspice

¼ teaspoon nutmeg

2 cups Basic Meat or Poultry Stock (page 225),
   made from beef

¼ cup arrowroot powder

¼ cup heavy cream

FOR THE NOODLES

3 tablespoons olive oil

6 zucchini, ends cut flat and spiralized
   into ribboned noodles

CONTINUED

TO MAKE THE MEATBALLS

1. In a large sauté pan, heat 3 tablespoons of the olive oil over medium-high heat until it shimmers.

2. Add the onion and cook, stirring occasionally, until it is soft, about 5 minutes.

3. Add the garlic and cook, stirring constantly, until it is fragrant, 30 to 60 seconds. Allow the onion and garlic to cool.

4. In a large bowl, combine the onion and garlic, ground beef, ground pork, almond meal, egg yolks, thyme, pepper, salt, allspice, and nutmeg. Mix well.

5. Form into 1-inch meatballs.

6. Heat the remaining 3 tablespoons of olive oil in a large sauté pan or skillet over medium-high heat.

7. Cook the meatballs, turning occasionally, until cooked through, about 10 minutes. Remove the meatballs and set aside.

8. Add 1½ cups of the beef stock to the pan, scraping any browned bits from the bottom of the pan with the side of a spoon.

9. Reduce the heat to medium. In a small bowl, whisk together the remaining ½ cup of beef stock with the arrowroot powder. Add to the sauté pan along with the heavy cream.

10. Cook, stirring frequently, until the sauce thickens, about 1 minute.

11. Return the meatballs to the pan to coat with the sauce.

TO MAKE THE NOODLES

In a large sauté pan, heat the olive oil over medium-high heat until it shimmers. Cook the noodles in the olive oil until they are al dente, about 5 minutes.

Cooking tip: *Depending on the size skillet you use, you may need to work in batches to cook the meatballs. Don't overcrowd the pan, or you'll wind up steaming the meatballs and keeping them from forming the flavorful caramelized crust you get with high-heat cooking.*

BEEF STEW
WITH CELERIAC EGG NOODLES

PREP TIME: 20 MINUTES / COOK TIME: 10 HOURS

 IDEAL FOR HAND-CRANK
SPIRALIZERS

- Straight blade
- Blade A

SERVES 4

GLUTEN-FREE,
PALEO-FRIENDLY

PER SERVING: Calories: 477;
Total Fat: 18g; Saturated Fat: 4g;
Cholesterol: 101mg;
Total Carbs: 29g; Fiber: 6g;
Protein: 42g

Spiralizer alternative: *If you do
not have a hand-crank spiralizer, use a vegetable peeler to
make the celeriac into noodles.*

*This hearty beef stew is ready when you get home because you
make it in the slow cooker. All you need to do is spend about
5 minutes putting together your egg noodles and warming
them up, and you're ready to go.*

FOR THE STEW

1 pound beef chuck, cut into 1-inch pieces

1 onion, chopped

3 carrots, chopped

1 celery stalk, chopped

1 pound button mushrooms, halved

4 garlic cloves, chopped

1 cup dry red wine

1 cup Basic Meat or Poultry Stock (page 225),
   made from beef

1 teaspoon dried thyme

1 teaspoon onion powder

1 teaspoon dried rosemary

1 teaspoon sea salt

¼ teaspoon freshly ground black pepper

FOR THE NOODLES

3 tablespoons olive oil

2 celeriac, greens removed, peeled, ends cut flat,
   and spiralized into ribboned noodles

2 tablespoons chopped fresh parsley

Put all of the ingredients in a 6-quart slow cooker. Cook, covered, on low, for 8 to 10 hours, until the meat is tender.

TO MAKE THE NOODLES

1. In a large sauté pan, heat the olive oil over medium-high heat until it shimmers.

2. Add the noodles and cook, stirring frequently, until al dente, 5 to 7 minutes.

3. Stir in the parsley.

4. Serve the stew over the noodles.

SLOW COOKER PORK, FENNEL, RED ONION, AND CABBAGE
OVER APPLE NOODLES

PREP TIME: 20 MINUTES / COOK TIME: 10 HOURS

 IDEAL FOR HAND-CRANK
SPIRALIZERS

- Shredder blade
- Blade D

SERVES 4

GLUTEN-FREE,
PALEO-FRIENDLY

PER SERVING: Calories: 577;
Total Fat: 36g; Saturated Fat: 11g;
Cholesterol: 102mg;
Total Carbs: 39g; Fiber: 10g;
Protein: 29g

Spiralizer alternative: *If you
don't have the ability to make
the wide noodles on your
spiralizer, you can also use
a vegetable peeler to make
them.*

*With cabbage and apples in season in the fall, this makes the
perfect dish for a chilly autumn evening. While the recipe calls
for pork shoulder, you can also use country-style spare ribs.
Cooking it in the slow cooker makes this meal a snap.*

FOR THE PORK

1 pound pork shoulder, cut into 1-inch pieces

1 fennel bulb, chopped

½ head cabbage, chopped

1 red onion, sliced

¼ cup apple cider vinegar

1 cup Basic Meat or Poultry Stock (page 225),
    made from chicken

1 teaspoon ground cinnamon

1 teaspoon garlic powder

½ teaspoon dried sage

1 teaspoon sea salt

¼ teaspoon freshly ground black pepper

FOR THE NOODLES

3 tablespoons olive oil

4 apples, stemmed, cored, ends cut flat,
    and spiralized into wide noodles

1. In a 6-quart slow cooker, combine all of the ingredients.

2. Cover and cook on low for 8 to 10 hours.

TO MAKE THE APPLE NOODLES

1. In a large sauté pan, heat the olive oil over medium-high heat until it shimmers.

2. Add the apple noodles and cook, stirring frequently, until al dente, about 5 minutes.

Make it lighter: *If the apples are too high in carbs for you, you can replace them with zucchini.*

BROCCOLINI BEEF STIR-FRY

PREP TIME: 15 MINUTES / COOK TIME: 15 MINUTES

 HAND-CRANK
- Shredder blade
- Blade D

HOURGLASS
- Thin-cutting blade

SERVES 4

GLUTEN-FREE,
PALEO-FRIENDLY

PER SERVING: Calories: 491;
Total Fat: 20g; Saturated Fat: 13g;
Cholesterol: 62mg;
Total Carbs: 31g; Fiber: 6g;
Protein: 45g

A quick stir-fry is the perfect fast weeknight meal. You can put this one together in 30 minutes or less, and it's loaded with healthy veggies and lots of protein. If you can't find broccolini, then broccoli florets will work in their place.

3 tablespoons coconut oil

1 pound flank steak, cut into ½-inch thick strips

6 scallions (white and green parts), sliced

1 tablespoon grated ginger

1 red bell pepper, seeded and sliced

1 carrot, peeled, ends cut flat, and spiralized into spaghetti noodles

1 cup shredded bok choy

2 cups broccolini

3 garlic cloves, minced

2 tablespoons wheat-free tamari or coconut aminos

2 tablespoons rice vinegar

¼ teaspoon sesame oil

¼ cup Basic Meat or Poultry Stock (page 225), made from chicken

Pinch crushed red pepper flakes

¼ cup arrowroot powder

1. In a large sauté pan or wok, heat the coconut oil over medium-high heat until it shimmers.

2. Add the steak and cook, stirring frequently, until it is done, about 5 minutes. Remove from the oil with a slotted spoon and set aside.

3. Add the scallions, ginger, bell pepper, carrot noodles, bok choy, and broccolini to the hot oil and cook, stirring frequently, until the vegetables are crisp-tender, about 5 minutes.

4. Add the garlic and cook, stirring constantly, until it is fragrant, 30 to 60 seconds.

5. In a small bowl, whisk together the tamari, rice vinegar, sesame oil, chicken stock, red pepper flakes, and arrowroot powder. Add to the stir-fry. Cook until it is slightly thick, about 3 minutes.

Cooking tip: *The colder the meat is, the easier it is to cut into thin strips. Put the meat in the freezer for about 30 minutes before slicing it, for easier cutting.*

CHICKEN BIRYANI
ON JICAMA RICE

PREP TIME: 20 MINUTES PLUS 3 HOURS MARINATING TIME / COOK TIME: 20 MINUTES

IDEAL FOR HAND-CRANK SPIRALIZERS

- Shredder blade
- Blade D

SERVES 4

GLUTEN-FREE

PER SERVING: Calories: 415;
Total Fat: 20g; Saturated Fat: 12g;
Cholesterol: 105mg;
Total Carbs: 22g; Fiber: 10g;
Protein: 36g

Spiralizer alternative: *If you have an hourglass spiralizer, you can replace the jicama with 2 large, peeled carrots.*

This rice dish from Northern India has such fragrant spices, it's really warming and flavorful. There are many different types of biryani, all with slight variances depending on where on the subcontinent they originate, but all are flavorful main dishes. Typical biryani is layered and baked. This one is a simple one-pot meal.

½ cup plain unsweetened yogurt

2 tablespoons curry powder

½ teaspoon ground cinnamon

1 pound boneless skinless chicken breast, cut into 1-inch cubes

1 medium jicama, peeled, ends cut flat, and spiralized into spaghetti noodles

3 tablespoons coconut oil

1 onion, chopped

1 tablespoon grated ginger

3 garlic cloves, minced

½ cup Basic Meat or Poultry Stock (page 225), made from chicken

3 tablespoons chopped fresh cilantro

1. In a medium bowl, mix together yogurt, curry powder, and cinnamon. Add the chicken and coat entirely with the marinade. Cover and let marinate in the refrigerator for 3 hours.

2. In the bowl of a food processor fitted with a chopping blade, pulse the jicama until it resembles rice, about 10 one-second pulses. Set aside.

3. In large sauté pan, heat the coconut oil over medium-high heat.

4. Add the onion and ginger and cook, stirring occasionally, until the onion is soft, about 5 minutes.

5. Add the garlic and cook, stirring constantly, until it is fragrant, 30 to 60 seconds.

6. Add the chicken and marinade and cook, stirring frequently, until chicken is cooked, about 10 minutes.

7. Add the chicken stock and jicama rice. Cook, stirring frequently, until the rice is soft, about 5 minutes.

8. Stir in the cilantro.

GROUND PORK STIR-FRY
WITH CABBAGE NOODLES

PREP TIME: 15 MINUTES / COOK TIME: 20 MINUTES

IDEAL FOR HAND-CRANK
SPIRALIZERS

- Chipper blade
- Blade B

SERVES 4

GLUTEN-FREE,
PALEO-FRIENDLY

PER SERVING: Calories: 243;
Total Fat: 5g; Saturated Fat: 2g;
Cholesterol: 83mg;
Total Carbs: 16g; Fiber: 4g;
Protein: 32g

Spiralizer alternative: *If your
spiralizer won't handle cabbage, you can shred it on a
box grater instead.*

*Ground pork has lots of fat, so it makes a great base for a stir-
fry. Remove the pork from the fat with a slotted spoon, and then
cook the vegetables in the fat that remains. Choose either green
or colorful red cabbage for this dish.*

1 pound ground pork

6 scallions (white and green parts), chopped

1 teaspoon grated ginger

1 carrot, peeled and chopped

1 red bell pepper, seeded and chopped

½ medium cabbage, cored, outer
    leaves removed, and spiralized into
    fettuccine noodles

4 garlic cloves, minced

2 tablespoons rice vinegar

1 tablespoon wheat-free tamari or
    coconut aminos

¼ teaspoon chili oil

2 tablespoons fresh orange juice

2 tablespoons arrowroot powder

1. In a large sauté pan or wok on medium-high heat, cook
the pork, crumbling with a spoon, until browned, about
5 minutes. Remove the pork with a slotted spoon and
set aside.

2. In the pork fat, cook the scallions, ginger, carrot, red bell
pepper, and cabbage noodles, stirring occasionally, until it is
crisp-tender, about 5 minutes.

3. Add the garlic and cook, stirring constantly, until it is fragrant, 30 to 60 seconds.

4. Return the pork to the pan.

5. In a small bowl, whisk together the rice vinegar, tamari, chili oil, orange juice, and arrowroot powder.

6. Add the sauce to the stir-fry and cook until it thickens slightly, about 3 minutes.

ORANGE BEEF
ON FRIED SWEET POTATO RICE

PREP TIME: 10 MINUTES / COOK TIME: 20 MINUTES

 IDEAL FOR HAND-CRANK
SPIRALIZERS
- Shredder blade
- Blade D

SERVES 4

GLUTEN-FREE,
PALEO-FRIENDLY

PER SERVING: Calories: 389;
Total Fat: 21g; Saturated Fat: 13g;
Cholesterol: 62mg;
Total Carbs: 17g; Fiber: 2g;
Protein: 35g

Spiralizer alternative: *An hour-glass spiralizer will not work for the sweet potato. Instead, thinly slice the potato with a mandoline or a sharp knife.*

This sweet and spicy orange sauce is the perfect complement to the beef, broccoli, and sweet potato rice. Use a beef that stays tender, such as flank steak, and cut it against the grain. Doing so shortens the fibers in the meat, making it more tender.

2 sweet potatoes, peeled, ends cut flat,
 and spiralized into spaghetti noodles
3 tablespoons coconut oil
1 pound flank steak, cut into ½-inch thick strips
5 scallions (white and green parts), sliced
2 cups broccoli florets
4 ounces shiitake mushrooms, sliced
2 garlic cloves, minced
Zest of 1 orange, plus ½ cup fresh squeezed
 orange juice
½ teaspoon chili oil
2 tablespoons wheat-free tamari
 or coconut aminos
2 tablespoons arrowroot powder

1. In the bowl of a food processor fitted with a chopping blade, pulse the sweet potato noodles until it resembles rice, 10 to 20 one-second pulses.

2. In a large sauté pan or wok, heat the coconut oil over medium-high heat until it shimmers.

3. Add the steak and cook, stirring frequently, until it is done, about 5 minutes. Remove the steak from the oil with a slotted spoon and set aside.

4. Add the scallions, broccoli, and mushrooms to the oil in the pan. Cook, stirring frequently, until the vegetables are soft, about 5 minutes.

5. Add the reserved sweet potato rice and cook, stirring frequently, for 4 minutes.

6. Add the garlic and cook, until it is fragrant, stirring constantly, 30 to 60 seconds.

7. In a small bowl, whisk together the orange zest and juice, chili oil, tamari, and arrowroot powder. Add them to the stir-fry.

8. Cook, stirring frequently, until the rice is al dente, another 3 or 4 minutes.

9. Return the reserved steak to the pan. Cook until it is warm, 1 or 2 minutes.

LAMB KAFTA KEBAB
WITH MOROCCAN–SPICED CARROT RICE

PREP TIME: 20 MINUTES / COOK TIME: 20 MINUTES

 HAND-CRANK

- Shredder blade
- Blade D

HOURGLASS

- Thin-cutting blade

SERVES 4

GLUTEN-FREE,
PALEO-FRIENDLY

PER SERVING: Calories: 373;
Total Fat: 20g; Saturated Fat: 5g;
Cholesterol: 102mg;
Total Carbs: 16g; Fiber: 5g;
Protein: 34g

Shish kebab in Turkish means, "cooked on a skewer." These kebab skewers are made the traditional way, with lamb coated in Middle Eastern spices. While you can grill the kebab on the stovetop or outdoors, this recipe allows you to bake them. Serve them over carrot rice to add a modern twist to a very old recipe.

FOR THE KEBAB

1 pound ground lamb

1 onion, finely chopped

3 garlic cloves, minced

2 tablespoons fresh mint, chopped

2 tablespoons fresh oregano, chopped

2 tablespoons chopped fresh flat-leaf parsley

2 teaspoons ground cumin

2 teaspoons smoked paprika

½ teaspoon ground cinnamon

2 teaspoons ground coriander

½ teaspoon sea salt

FOR THE RICE

6 carrots, peeled, ends cut flat,
    and spiralized into spaghetti noodles

3 tablespoons olive oil

1 teaspoon ground coriander

1 teaspoon ground cumin

½ teaspoon cinnamon

Garlic Aioli (page 229) (optional)

1. Preheat your oven to 350°F.

2. Line a baking sheet with parchment paper.

3. In a large bowl, combine all of the kebab ingredients, mixing thoroughly.

4. Divide the meat evenly into 16 pieces. Shape each piece around a soaked wooden skewer.

5. Bake on the parchment-lined baking sheet in the pre-heated oven until the meat is browned, about 17 minutes.

TO MAKE THE RICE

1. In the bowl of a food processor fitted with a chopping blade, pulse the carrot noodles until it resembles rice, about 10 one-second pulses.

2. In a large sauté pan, heat the olive oil, coriander, cumin, and cinnamon.

3. Add the carrot rice and cook, stirring occasionally, until it is al dente, about 5 minutes.

4. Serve the kebab on top of the rice with garlic aioli (if using).

Cooking tip: *Soak wooden skewers for at least 6 hours before using on the grill or in the oven.*

DIRTY RICE

PREP TIME: 20 MINUTES / COOK TIME: 20 MINUTES

IDEAL FOR HAND-CRANK
SPIRALIZERS
- Shredder blade
- Blade D

SERVES 4

GLUTEN-FREE,
PALEO-FRIENDLY

PER SERVING: Calories: 311;
Total Fat: 15g; Saturated Fat: 4;
Cholesterol: 370mg;
Total Carbs: 12g; Fiber: 3g;
Protein: 33g

Spiralizer alternative: *If you do
not have a hand-crank spiralizer, cut the celeriac into thin
pieces with a paring knife and
process until it resembles rice.*

*This Creole dish is called "dirty" because small pieces of chicken
liver, meat, and vegetables dirty up the pristine color of the white
rice. The flavor, however, is anything but dirty. It's wonderfully
spiced and soulfully satisfying.*

2 celeriac, greens removed, peeled, ends cut flat,
    and spiralized into spaghetti noodles
½ pound ground beef
½ pound chicken livers, chopped
2 tablespoons olive oil
½ onion, chopped
1 carrot, chopped
1 celery stalk, chopped
½ green pepper, chopped
2 garlic cloves, minced
½ teaspoon sea salt
¼ teaspoon freshly ground black pepper
2 tablespoons chopped fresh parsley

1. In a food processor fitted with a chopping blade, pulse the
celeriac noodles until it resembles rice, about 10 one-second
pulses. Set aside.

2. In a large sauté pan, cook the ground beef and livers,
crumbling the beef with the side of the spoon, until browned,
5 to 7 minutes. Remove them from the fat with a slotted
spoon and set them aside.

3. In the same sauté pan, add the olive oil and heat until it
shimmers. Add the onion, carrot, celery, and green pepper.
Cook, stirring occasionally, until vegetables are soft, about
5 minutes.

4. Add the reserved rice and cook, stirring occasionally, until it is tender, about 5 minutes.

5. Add the garlic and cook, stirring constantly, until it is fragrant, 30 to 60 seconds.

6. Add the reserved chicken livers and ground beef along with the salt, pepper, and parsley. Cook to heat through, 2 minutes more.

MOROCCAN GROUND LAMB
WITH CARROT NOODLES

PREP TIME: 10 MINUTES / COOK TIME: 20 MINUTES

HAND-CRANK
- Shredder blade
- Blade D

HOURGLASS
- Thin-cutting blade

SERVES 4

GLUTEN-FREE,
PALEO-FRIENDLY

PER SERVING: Calories: 356;
Total Fat: 19g; Saturated Fat: 5g;
Cholesterol: 102mg;
Total Carbs: 13g; Fiber: 3g;
Protein: 33g

As the lamb cooks, your house will fill with incredible scents of cumin and cinnamon. This quick stir-fry is extremely easy.

1 pound ground lamb
3 tablespoons olive oil
1 teaspoon ground cumin
½ teaspoon ground cinnamon
1 teaspoon ground coriander
1 onion, chopped
6 carrots, peeled, ends cut flat,
    and spiralized into spaghetti noodles
3 garlic cloves, chopped
3 tablespoons chopped fresh cilantro

1. In a large sauté pan, cook the ground lamb, crumbling it with a spoon, until browned, about 5 minutes. Remove the lamb from the fat with a slotted spoon and set it aside.

2. In the same pan, add the olive oil and warm until it shimmers. Add the cumin, cinnamon, coriander, and onion. Cook, stirring occasionally, until the onion is soft, about 5 minutes.

3. Add the carrot noodles and cook, stirring frequently, until they are soft, another 5 minutes. Add the garlic and cook, stirring constantly, until it is fragrant, 30 to 60 seconds. Stir in the cilantro.

> **Substitution tip:** *You can also make this with ground beef or even ground pork.*

SLOW COOKER BEEF SHORT RIBS
ON CABBAGE NOODLES

PREP TIME: 10 MINUTES / COOK TIME: 10 HOURS

IDEAL FOR HAND-CRANK
SPIRALIZERS
- Chipper blade
- Blade B

SERVES 4

GLUTEN-FREE,
PALEO-FRIENDLY

PER SERVING: Calories: 439;
Total Fat: 10g; Saturated Fat: 4g;
Cholesterol: 103mg;
Total Carbs: 16g; Fiber: 2g;
Protein: 35g

Red wine makes the perfect braising medium for fatty, delicious short ribs. Choose a dry red wine (Syrah, Pinot Noir, or Cabernet Sauvignon) to cut through the fattiness of the beef.

FOR THE SHORT RIBS

1 pound beef short ribs

1 onion, chopped

2 carrots, peeled and chopped

6 garlic cloves, sliced

8 ounces crimini mushrooms, quartered

750 mL (1 bottle) dry red wine

1 teaspoon dried thyme

2 tablespoons prepared hot horseradish

1 teaspoon sea salt

½ teaspoon fresh ground black pepper

FOR THE CABBAGE NOODLES

1 medium cabbage, cored, outer leaves removed,
   and spiralized into fettuccine noodles

3 tablespoons olive oil

TO MAKE THE SHORT RIBS

1. In a 6-quart slow cooker, combine all of the ingredients.

2. Cook on low, covered, for 8 to 10 hours.

TO MAKE THE CABBAGE NOODLES

1. In a large sauté pan, heat the olive oil over medium-high heat until it shimmers.

2. Add the cabbage noodles and cook, stirring frequently, until soft, 4 to 6 minutes.

3. Serve the short ribs and sauce over the cabbage noodles.

MEAT AND VEGGIE MUFFINS

PREP TIME: 15 MINUTES / COOK TIME: 20 MINUTES

HAND-CRANK

- Shredder blade
- Blade D

HOURGLASS

- Thin-cutting blade

SERVES 4

GLUTEN-FREE,
PALEO-FRIENDLY

PER SERVING: Calories: 371;
Total Fat: 20g; Saturated Fat: 9g;
Cholesterol: 133mg;
Total Carbs: 11g; Fiber: 4g;
Protein: 39g

Meatloaf by any other name, these meat and veggie muffins are small so they cook much more quickly than meatloaf. That means you can get them on the table faster. Serve with one of the delicious salads from the salads chapter, as well as a side of homemade Ketchup (page 230).

1 zucchini, ends cut flat and spiralized
   into spaghetti noodles

1 carrot, peeled, ends cut flat,
   and spiralized into spaghetti

½ pound ground beef

½ pound ground pork

½ onion, finely chopped

2 garlic cloves, minced

1 teaspoon dried thyme

1 tablespoon Dijon mustard

1 tablespoon Worcestershire sauce

1 teaspoon homemade Sriracha (page 228)
   or store-bought

1 egg, beaten

½ cup almond milk

½ cup almond meal

1 teaspoon salt

½ teaspoon freshly ground black pepper

Homemade Ketchup (page 230) (optional)

1. Preheat the oven to 450°F.

2. In the bowl of a food processor fitted with a chopping blade, pulse the zucchini and carrot noodles until they resemble rice, about 20 one-second pulses.

3. In a large bowl, combine the carrot and zucchini rice with the ground beef, ground pork, onion, garlic, mustard, Worcestershire sauce, sriracha, egg, almond milk, almond meal, salt, and pepper. Mix well with your hands.

4. Fill each muffin of a 12-muffin tin with the meatloaf mixture. Bake in the preheated oven for 20 minutes, or until done.

Substitution tip: *You can make this meatloaf from 1 pound of ground beef and eliminate the ground pork entirely, if you wish.*

SPICY ASIAN ZUCCHINI NOODLES
WITH PORK AND PEANUT SAUCE

PREP TIME: 15 MINUTES, PLUS 4 HOURS MARINATING / COOK TIME: 25 MINUTES

HAND-CRANK
- Shredder blade
- Blade D

HOURGLASS
- Thin-cutting blade

SERVES 4

GLUTEN-FREE

PER SERVING: Calories: 657;
Total Fat: 51g; Saturated Fat: 21g;
Cholesterol: 62mg;
Total Carbs: 19g; Fiber: 6g;
Protein: 35g

Peanut sauce is the perfect sauce for zoodles, coating them with fatty, nutty goodness. The peanut sauce tempers the heat, while the pork adds extra protein for a healthy, balanced meal.

FOR THE PORK

¼ cup olive oil

1 teaspoons sesame oil

½ teaspoon chili oil

¼ cup rice vinegar

2 tablespoons wheat-free tamari
   or coconut aminos

12 ounces pork tenderloin

2 tablespoons coconut oil

FOR THE NOODLES

3 tablespoons coconut oil

¼ teaspoon chili oil

3 scallions, sliced

1 tablespoon grated ginger

6 zucchini, ends cut flat and spiralized
   into spaghetti noodles

3 garlic cloves, minced

1 cup Nut Butter Sauce (page 231), made
   with peanut butter

2 tablespoons chopped fresh cilantro

TO MAKE THE PORK

1. In a small bowl, whisk together the olive oil, sesame oil, chili oil, rice vinegar, and tamari.

2. In a large zipper bag, combine the pork with the marinade. Marinate for at least 4 hours and up to 10 hours.

3. Preheat the oven to 425°F.

4. In a large ovenproof skillet, heat the coconut oil over medium-high heat.

5. Remove the pork from the marinade and pat it dry with paper towels.

6. Sear the tenderloin on all sides, about 3 minutes per side.

7. Transfer the tenderloin to the preheated oven and roast until the internal temperature registers 145°F, about 15 to 20 minutes. Rest, tented with foil, for 20 minutes.

8. Cut the tenderloin into ½-inch thick slices.

TO MAKE THE NOODLES

1. In a large sauté pan, heat the coconut oil and chili oil over medium-high heat.

2. Add the scallions, ginger, and zucchini noodles. Cook, stirring frequently, until zucchini is tender, about 5 minutes.

3. Add the garlic and cook, stirring constantly, until it is fragrant, 30 to 60 seconds.

4. Stir in the nut butter sauce, cooking until it is warmed through, about 1 minute.

5. Stir in the cilantro, and serve the noodles topped with the tenderloin.

LINGUICA, PEPPERS, AND JICAMA RICE

PREP TIME: 15 MINUTES / COOK TIME: 20 MINUTES

IDEAL FOR HAND-CRANK SPIRALIZERS

- Shredder blade
- Blade D

SERVES 4

GLUTEN-FREE, PALEO-FRIENDLY

PER SERVING: Calories: 548; Total Fat: 37g; Saturated Fat: 11g; Cholesterol: 80mg; Total Carbs: 31g; Fiber: 13g; Protein: 23g

Spiralizer alternative: *If you have an hourglass spiralizer, you can replace the jicama with 2 large, peeled carrots.*

Linguica is a Portuguese sausage seasoned with paprika and garlic. Choose the linguica that comes in casings for this recipe. You can find linguica in the meat department of most grocery stores. If you can't find it, feel free to substitute your favorite smoked sausage.

1 medium jicama, peeled, ends cut flat, and spiralized into spaghetti noodles
2 tablespoons olive oil
1 pound linguica, cut into 1-inch pieces
½ onion, chopped
½ red pepper, seeded and chopped
½ yellow pepper, seeded and chopped
½ green pepper, seeded and chopped
3 garlic cloves, minced
1 (14-ounce) can crushed tomatoes, undrained
1 tablespoon smoked paprika
½ teaspoon sea salt
¼ teaspoon freshly ground black pepper

1. In the bowl of a food processor fitted with a chopping blade, pulse the jicama noodles until it resembles rice, about 10 one-second pulses. Set aside.

2. In a large pot, heat the olive oil over medium-high heat until it shimmers.

3. Add the linguica and cook, stirring occasionally, until cooked through, 5 to 7 minutes. Remove the linguica from the pot with a slotted spoon and set it aside.

4. In the same pot, add the onion, red pepper, yellow pepper, and green pepper. Cook, stirring occasionally, until vegetables are soft, about 5 minutes.

5. Add the garlic cloves and cook, stirring constantly, until it is fragrant, 30 to 60 seconds.

6. Add the crushed tomatoes, smoked paprika, salt, pepper, reserved jicama rice, and reserved linguica.

7. Cook, stirring occasionally, until the rice is tender, about 5 minutes.

CHORIZO AND TOMATO JICAMA RICE WITH AVOCADO

PREP TIME: 15 MINUTES / COOK TIME: 20 MINUTES

 IDEAL FOR HAND-CRANK
SPIRALIZERS

- Shredder blade
- Blade D

SERVES 4

GLUTEN-FREE,
PALEO-FRIENDLY

PER SERVING: Calories: 781;
Total Fat: 60g; Saturated Fat: 20g;
Cholesterol: 100mg;
Total Carbs: 29g; Fiber: 14g;
Protein: 36g

Spiralizer alternative: *If you
have an hourglass spiralizer,
you can replace the jicama with
2 large, peeled carrots.*

*Chorizo is a spiced Latin-American pork sausage that tends
to have some heat to it. It's made with smoked red peppers and
chilies, making it pretty zippy. Fortunately, sliced avocado cools
down the heat significantly, giving this dish a lovely balance.*

1 medium jicama, peeled, ends cut flat,
    and spiralized into spaghetti noodles
2 tablespoons olive oil
1 pound chorizo, cut into 1-inch pieces
1 onion, chopped
1 carrot, chopped
3 garlic cloves, minced
1 (14-ounce) can tomatoes and peppers
    (such as Ro-Tel), undrained
1 teaspoon dried oregano
1 avocado, cut into cubes

1. In a food processor fitted with a chopping blade, pulse the
jicama noodles until it resembles rice, about 10 one-second
pulses. Set aside.

2. In a large pot, heat the olive oil until it shimmers. Add
the chorizo and cook until cooked through, 5 to 7 minutes.
Remove the sausage from the fat with a slotted spoon and set
it aside.

3. In the same pot, cook the onion and carrot, stirring occasionally, until they begin to brown, 5 to 7 minutes.

4. Add the garlic and cook, stirring constantly, until it is
fragrant, 30 to 60 seconds.

5. Stir in the tomatoes and peppers, scraping any browned bits from the bottom of the pan with the side of the spoon.

6. Add the oregano, reserved chorizo, and jicama rice. Cook, stirring frequently, until the jicama is soft, about 5 minutes.

7. Serve topped with the avocado cubes.

Cooking tip: *If you want to cool the heat even further, top the stew with a few tablespoons of sour cream and a few tablespoons of grated cheese.*

CARBONARA ON SUMMER SQUASH SPAGHETTI

PREP TIME: 10 MINUTES / COOK TIME: 15 MINUTES

HAND-CRANK
- Shredder blade
- Blade D

HOURGLASS
- Thin-cutting blade

SERVES 4

GLUTEN-FREE

PER SERVING: Calories: 567;
Total Fat: 47g; Saturated Fat: 17g;
Cholesterol: 161mg;
Total Carbs: 12g; Fiber: 3g;
Protein: 28g

This Italian dish comes from Rome, and it is essentially bacon and egg pasta. Of course, a nice helping of cream and cheese adds richness, making this humble and easy to prepare dish taste decadent. This recipe uses an uncured Italian bacon, pancetta, although you can replace it with American bacon if you wish.

FOR THE PASTA

3 tablespoons olive oil

6 yellow summer squash, ends cut flat
    and spiralized into spaghetti noodles

FOR THE CARBONARA

2 tablespoons olive oil

4 ounces pancetta, diced

1 shallot, minced

4 garlic cloves, minced

2 eggs, beaten

2 tablespoons heavy cream

6 ounces Asiago cheese, grated

Dash crushed red pepper flakes

¼ teaspoon freshly ground black pepper

2 tablespoons chopped fresh flat-leaf parsley

TO MAKE THE PASTA

1. In a large sauté pan, heat the olive oil over medium-high heat until it shimmers.

2. Add the squash and cook, stirring occasionally, until it is al dente, about 5 minutes

1. In a large sauté pan, heat the olive oil over medium-high heat until it shimmers.

2. Add the pancetta and shallot and cook, stirring occasionally until the pancetta is browned, about 5 minutes.

3. Add the garlic and cook, stirring constantly, until it is fragrant, 30 to 60 seconds.

4. Add the cooked squash noodles to the pan and remove it from the heat.

5. In a small bowl, whisk together the eggs, heavy cream, cheese, red pepper flakes, and pepper. Stir the mixture into the hot noodles, allowing the heat of the noodles to slightly cook and thicken the eggs.

6. Stir in the parsley.

9

CLASSIC
CRAVINGS

MEAT LOVER'S PIZZA PASTA

PREP TIME: 10 MINUTES / COOK TIME: 30 MINUTES

HAND-CRANK
- Chipper blade
- Blade B

HOURGLASS
- Thick-cutting blade

SERVES 4

GLUTEN-FREE

PER SERVING: Calories: 744;
Total Fat: 50g; Saturated Fat: 19g;
Cholesterol: 130mg;
Total Carbs: 29g; Fiber: 9g;
Protein: 48g

People on gluten-free and low-carb diets often talk about missing pizza. If it's the toppings you love, then try this pasta version, with spiralized zucchini noodles. It gives all of the flavor of pizza without the carbs or gluten.

FOR THE PASTA

4 zucchini, ends cut flat and spiralized
    into fettuccine noodles

Sea salt

FOR THE MARINARA

2 tablespoons olive oil

1 shallot, finely minced

4 garlic cloves, finely minced

2 (14-ounce) cans crushed tomatoes, undrained

1 tablespoon dried basil

1 tablespoon dried oregano

⅛ teaspoon crushed red pepper flakes

½ teaspoon sea salt

¼ teaspoon freshly ground black pepper

FOR THE PIZZA PASTA

4 ounces Italian sausage, crumbled and browned

4 ounces Canadian bacon, sliced into ribbons

4 ounces sliced pepperoni, sliced into ribbons

4 ounces sliced Genoa salami, sliced into ribbons

6 ounces mozzarella, grated

2 ounces Parmesan cheese, grated

TO MAKE THE PASTA

1. In a large colander over the sink, salt the zucchini noodles with the salt.

2. Allow the noodles to sit for 30 minutes to draw away as much water as possible.

3. Give the noodles a quick rinse and pat them dry with paper towels, wiping away any excess salt.

TO MAKE THE MARINARA

1. In a large sauté pan, heat the olive oil over medium-high heat until it shimmers.

2. Add the shallots and cook, stirring occasionally, until they are soft, about 4 minutes.

3. Add the garlic and cook, stirring constantly, until it is fragrant, 30 to 60 seconds.

4. Add the tomatoes, basil, oregano, red pepper flakes, salt, and pepper. Simmer on medium-low heat until the sauce thickens slightly, about 5 minutes more.

TO MAKE THE PIZZA PASTA

1. Preheat your oven to 375°F.

2. In a large bowl, toss together the zucchini noodles, marinara sauce, Italian sausage, Canadian bacon, pepperoni, and salami.

3. Put the mixture into a 9-by-9-inch baking pan.

4. Sprinkle with the mozzarella and Parmesan cheeses.

5. Bake in the preheated oven until the cheese is bubbly, about 20 minutes.

> **Make it lighter:** *If you want to make this recipe vegetarian, eliminate the meat. Instead, substitute sautéed red and green bell peppers and mushrooms.*

SPAGHETTI AND MEATBALLS

PREP TIME: 10 MINUTES / COOK TIME: 40 MINUTES

HAND-CRANK
- Chipper blade
- Blade B

HOURGLASS
- Thick-cutting blade

SERVES 4

GLUTEN-FREE,
PALEO-FRIENDLY

PER SERVING: Calories: 558;
Total Fat: 32g; Saturated Fat: 6g;
Cholesterol: 135mg;
Total Carbs: 29g; Fiber: 11g;
Protein: 44g

Pasta is pretty hard to give up when you cut out the carbs. One of the most popular pasta dishes, spaghetti and meatballs, gets an easy low-carb makeover with this recipe. Use zucchini noodles or replace with any noodles from your favorite spiralizable veggie.

FOR THE PASTA

4 zucchini, ends cut flat and spiralized
    into fettuccine noodles

Sea salt

3 tablespoons olive oil

FOR THE MEATBALLS

½ pound ground pork

½ pound ground beef

½ cup almond meal

3 garlic cloves, minced

2 tablespoons finely minced shallot

1 egg, beaten

1 tablespoon Italian seasoning

FOR THE MARINARA

2 tablespoons olive oil

1 shallot, finely minced

4 garlic cloves, finely minced

2 (14-ounce) cans crushed tomatoes, undrained

1 tablespoon dried basil

1 tablespoon dried oregano

⅛ teaspoon crushed red pepper flakes

½ teaspoon sea salt

¼ teaspoon freshly ground black pepper

1. In a large colander over the sink, salt the zucchini noodles with the sea salt.

2. Allow the noodles to sit for 30 minutes to draw away as much water as possible.

3. Give the noodles a quick rinse and pat them dry with paper towels, wiping away any excess salt.

4. In a large sauté pan, heat the olive oil over medium-high heat until it shimmers.

5. Add the noodles and cook, stirring occasionally, until soft, about 5 minutes.

TO MAKE THE MEATBALLS

1. Preheat the oven to 400°F.

2. Line a baking sheet with parchment paper.

3. In a large bowl, combine all of the meatball ingredients, mixing with your hands until well mixed.

4. Roll the meat mixture into 1-inch balls. Put them on the prepared baking sheet. Bake until the meatballs are cooked, 20 to 25 minutes.

TO MAKE THE MARINARA

1. In a large sauté pan, heat the olive oil over medium-high heat until it shimmers.

2. Add the shallot and cook, stirring occasionally, until soft, about 4 minutes.

CONTINUED

Spaghetti and Meatballs, *continued*

3. Add the garlic and cook, stirring constantly, until it is fragrant, 30 to 60 seconds.

4. Add the tomatoes, basil, oregano, red pepper flakes, salt, and pepper. Simmer on medium-low heat until the sauce thickens slightly, about 5 minutes more.

5. Serve the sauce on top of the noodles, with the meatballs on top.

TUNA NOODLE CASSEROLE

PREP TIME: 15 MINUTES / COOK TIME: 35 MINUTES

IDEAL FOR HAND-CRANK
SPIRALIZERS

- Straight blade
- Blade A

SERVES 4

GLUTEN-FREE,
PALEO-FRIENDLY

PER SERVING: Calories: 432;
Total Fat: 30g; Saturated Fat: 15g;
Cholesterol: 90mg;
Total Carbs: 17g; Fiber: 5g;
Protein: 27g

Spiralizer alternative: *If you
don't have a spiralizer that
will make wide noodles, use
a vegetable peeler to cut the
zucchini into strips. Or your
hourglass-shaped spiralizer can
make fettuccine noodles using
the thick-cutting blade, instead.*

*If you always loved Mom's tuna noodle casserole, then this
lower-carbohydrate version will be certain to satisfy your craving for this classic comfort food. While many tuna casseroles
have peas in them, they tend to be a bit high in carbs. Feel free
to add them if you wish (about a quarter cup), but to save carbs
this recipe leaves them out.*

FOR THE NOODLES

4 zucchini, ends cut flat and spiralized
   into ribboned noodles

Sea salt

FOR THE CASSEROLE

5 tablespoons melted butter, divided

1 onion, chopped

1 celery stalk, minced

8 ounces crimini mushrooms, sliced

2 (5-ounce) cans chunk tuna, packed in water,
   drained

2 garlic cloves, minced

1 cup Basic Meat or Poultry Stock (page 225),
   made with chicken

1 teaspoon dried thyme

1 teaspoon onion powder

1 teaspoon garlic powder

1 teaspoon sea salt

½ teaspoon freshly ground black pepper

¾ cup heavy cream

½ cup almond meal

CONTINUED

Tuna Noodle Casserole,
continued

TO MAKE THE NOODLES

1. Cut the zucchini noodles into 2-inch pieces.

2. In a large colander set over the sink, sprinkle salt over the noodles. Allow the salt to sit on the zucchini for 30 minutes to pull out as much water as possible.

3. Quickly rinse the noodles and pat them dry, removing any remaining salt crystals.

TO MAKE THE CASSEROLE

1. Preheat the oven to 400°F.

2. In a large sauté pan, heat 3 tablespoons of the butter over medium-high heat.

3. Add the onion, celery, and mushrooms and cook, stirring occasionally, until the vegetables are soft, about 5 minutes.

4. Add the tuna and cook, stirring occasionally, 4 minutes.

5. Add the garlic and cook, stirring constantly, until it is fragrant, 30 to 60 seconds.

6. Add the chicken stock, thyme, onion powder, garlic powder, salt, and pepper. Cook, stirring occasionally, until the liquid reduces by half, about 4 minutes.

7. Stir in the heavy cream and cook, stirring constantly, until warmed through, 3 to 4 minutes more.

8. Add the noodles to the mixture and remove it from the heat.

9. Pour the mixture into a 9-by-9-inch baking dish.

10. Bake in the preheated oven for 20 minutes.

11. In a small bowl, combine the remaining 2 tablespoons of butter with the almond meal, running it through your fingers to ensure it is well mixed.

12. Sprinkle the mixture on top of the casserole.

13. Bake for another 5 minutes.

FETTUCCINE ALFREDO

PREP TIME: 10 MINUTES / COOK TIME: 10 MINUTES

HAND-CRANK

- Chipper blade
- Blade B

HOURGLASS

- Thick-cutting blade

SERVES 4

GLUTEN-FREE, VEGETARIAN

PER SERVING: Calories: 488;
Total Fat: 47g; Saturated Fat: 24g;
Cholesterol: 109mg;
Total Carbs: 12g; Fiber: 3g;
Protein: 10g

Traditional Alfredo sauce starts with a roux of flour and butter, which adds gluten and carbs. This all-dairy version is higher in fat, but it's rich, decadent, and low in carbohydrates. It makes a great base sauce for all kinds of toppings or add-ins, making it a very versatile sauce.

FOR THE PASTA

6 zucchini, ends cut flat, and spiralized
   into fettuccine noodles
Sea salt
3 tablespoons olive oil

FOR THE SAUCE

8 ounces cream cheese, cubed
¼ cup unsalted butter
¼ cup heavy cream
½ cup grated Asiago cheese

TO MAKE THE PASTA

1. In a large colander over the sink, salt the zucchini noodles with the salt.

2. Allow the noodles to sit for 30 minutes to draw away as much water as possible.

3. Give the noodles a quick rinse and pat them dry with paper towels, wiping away any excess salt.

4. In a large sauté pan, heat the olive oil over medium-high heat until it shimmers.

5. Add the noodles and cook, stirring occasionally, until they are soft, about 5 minutes.

1. In a large saucepan, heat all sauce ingredients over medium heat, stirring constantly, until the cheese melts and the sauce is thick, about 5 minutes.

2. Serve the sauce on top of the pasta

Substitution tip: *Add meat or veggies to the pasta for more variety. Try some sautéed broccoli and mushrooms for a vegetarian version, or cook 8 ounces of chicken or shrimp for a meatier version.*

SHRIMP SCAMPI
ON ANGEL HAIR

PREP TIME: 15 MINUTES / COOK TIME: 15 MINUTES

 IDEAL FOR HAND-CRANK
SPIRALIZERS

- Angel hair blade
- Blade D

SERVES 4

GLUTEN-FREE,
PALEO-FRIENDLY

PER SERVING: Calories: 374;
Total Fat: 23g; Saturated Fat: 3g;
Cholesterol: 223mg;
Total Carbs: 14g; Fiber: 4g;
Protein: 29g

Spiralizer alternative: *If you
don't have a spiralizer that
makes angel hair, you can cut
your zoodles into spaghetti
noodles instead using a hand-
crank or hourglass-shaped
spiralizer.*

The word scampi *means "prawn." However, other types of
crustaceans, such as lobster, may be used in the preparation
of this classic dish. This one takes a literal approach, using
medium-sized shrimp as the base.*

FOR THE PASTA

3 tablespoons olive oil

6 zucchini, ends cut flat and spiralized
    into angel hair noodles

FOR THE SCAMPI

3 tablespoons olive oil

2 tablespoons shallot, finely minced

16 ounces medium shrimp, peeled, deveined,
    and tails removed

6 garlic cloves, minced

½ cup dry white wine

1 teaspoon lemon zest, plus 2 tablespoons
    lemon juice (fresh squeezed)

¼ teaspoon crushed red pepper flakes

½ teaspoon sea salt

¼ teaspoon freshly ground black pepper

3 tablespoons chopped fresh flat-leaf parsley

TO MAKE THE PASTA

1. In a large sauté pan over medium-high heat, heat the
olive oil until it shimmers.

2. Add the noodles and cook, stirring occasionally, until
al dente, about 5 minutes.

TO MAKE THE SCAMPI

1. In a large sauté pan over medium-high heat, heat the olive oil until it shimmers.

2. Add the shallot and cook, stirring occasionally, until it is soft, about 4 minutes.

3. Add the shrimp and cook, stirring occasionally, until the shrimp is pink, 4 to 5 minutes.

4. Add the garlic and cook, stirring constantly, until it is fragrant, 30 to 60 seconds.

5. Add the wine and cook for 2 minutes.

6. Add the lemon zest and juice, red pepper flakes, salt, and pepper and cook, stirring occasionally, another 4 minutes.

7. Add the zoodles and parsley and cook until warmed through, 1 to 2 minutes.

SPAGHETTI WITH CLASSIC PESTO SAUCE

PREP TIME: 10 MINUTES / COOK TIME: 5 MINUTES

 HAND-CRANK
- Shredder blade
- Blade D

HOURGLASS
- Thin-cutting blade

SERVES 4

GLUTEN-FREE,
PALEO-FRIENDLY,
VEGETARIAN

PER SERVING: Calories: 439;
Total Fat: 44g; Saturated Fat: 7g;
Cholesterol: 5mg; Total Carbs: 12g;
Fiber: 4g; Protein: 8g

Pesto is a delicious green sauce that originates in Genoa, Italy. While over the years people have used an array of different ingredients to make pesto, such as spinach, kale, walnuts, and other vegetables, the classic pesto has five ingredients plus salt and pepper: basil, olive oil, Parmesan cheese, pine nuts, and garlic.

FOR THE PASTA

6 zucchini, ends cut flat and spiralized
  into spaghetti noodles
Sea salt
3 tablespoons olive oil

FOR THE PESTO

2 cups fresh basil
3 garlic cloves
¼ cup pine nuts
½ cup extra virgin olive oil
½ cup Parmesan cheese
½ teaspoon sea salt
¼ teaspoon freshly ground black pepper

TO MAKE THE PASTA

1. In a large colander set over the sink, sprinkle salt over the noodles. Allow the salt to sit on the zucchini for 30 minutes to pull out as much water as possible.

2. In a large sauté pan over medium-high heat, heat the olive oil until it shimmers.

3. Add the noodles and cook, stirring occasionally, until al dente, about 5 minutes.

1. In the bowl of a food processor fitted with a chopping blade, combine all of the pesto ingredients.

2. Process until well-combined and chopped, 15 to 20 seconds.

3. Toss the pesto with the hot zoodles.

Substitution tip: *Using the proportions above, feel free to experiment with different types of greens or nuts, such as kale and almond pesto or spinach and walnut pesto. You can also try different types of hard cheeses, such as Asiago or Pecorino Romano cheese.*

BLT ON POTATO FRITTERS

PREP TIME: 20 MINUTES / COOK TIME: 20 MINUTES

IDEAL FOR HAND-CRANK
SPIRALIZERS

- Shredder blade
- Blade D

SERVES 2

GLUTEN-FREE

PER SERVING: Calories: 741;
Total Fat: 51g; Saturated Fat: 12g;
Cholesterol: 283mg;
Total Carbs: 50g; Fiber: 9g;
Protein: 27g

Spiralizer alternative: *An hour-glass spiralizer will not work for the potato. Instead, use a vegetable peeler to shave it into slices.*

Potato fritters serve as the bread in the tasty BLT sandwich. Select artisan thick-cut bacon and really fresh, in-season tomatoes for best results. The homemade garlic aioli adds a nice kick to these delicious classic sandwiches.

FOR THE FRITTERS

2 russet potatoes, peeled, ends cut flat,
  and spiralized into spaghetti noodles
3 scallions (white and green parts), finely chopped
¼ cup almond meal
¼ cup grated Asiago cheese
3 eggs, beaten
1 teaspoon garlic powder
1 teaspoon Dijon mustard
½ teaspoon sea salt
¼ teaspoon freshly ground black pepper
3 tablespoons olive oil

FOR THE SANDWICH

2 tablespoons Garlic Aioli (page 229)
4 slices thick cut bacon, cooked crisp and halved
2 heirloom tomatoes, sliced
4 large lettuce leaves

TO MAKE THE BREAD

1. In a bowl, combine the potato noodles, scallions, almond meal, cheese, eggs, garlic powder, mustard, salt, and pepper. Mix well.

2. In a nonstick skillet, heat the olive oil over medium heat until it shimmers. Form the potato mixture into four patties and put them in the hot oil.

3. As they cook, press the fritters down with the spatula to flatten them.

4. Cook for about 5 minutes per side, until they are cooked through.

5. Allow the fritters to cool slightly.

TO MAKE THE SANDWICHES

1. Spread two slices of the fritters with the garlic aioli.

2. Top the aioli with the tomatoes, four bacon pieces, a piece of lettuce, and another fritter on top.

BACON CHEESEBURGER
ON A POTATO FRITTER BUN

PREP TIME: 20 MINUTES / COOK TIME: 40 MINUTES

 IDEAL FOR HAND-CRANK
SPIRALIZERS
- Shredder blade
- Blade D

SERVES 4

GLUTEN-FREE

PER SERVING: Calories: 847;
Total Fat: 57g; Saturated Fat: 17g;
Cholesterol: 283mg;
Total Carbs: 24g; Fiber: 4g;
Protein: 61g

Spiralizer alternative: *An hour-glass spiralizer will not work for the sweet potato. Instead, use a vegetable peeler to shave it into slices.*

Sometimes you just need a cheeseburger. When that happens, make these delicious open-faced cheeseburgers on potato fritters. While this recipe calls for blue cheese crumbles, you can use your favorite type of cheese to make a tasty burger.

FOR THE BUN

2 russet potatoes, peeled, ends cut flat, and spiralized into spaghetti noodles
3 scallions (white and green parts), finely chopped
¼ cup almond meal
¼ cup grated Asiago cheese
3 eggs, beaten
1 teaspoon garlic powder
1 teaspoon Dijon mustard
½ teaspoon sea salt
¼ teaspoon freshly ground black pepper
3 tablespoons olive oil

FOR THE CARAMELIZED ONIONS

3 tablespoons extra virgin olive oil
1 onion, thinly sliced
½ teaspoon sea salt
½ teaspoon dried thyme

FOR THE BURGERS

1 pound ground beef
1 teaspoon fish sauce
3 garlic cloves, minced
½ teaspoon sea salt
¼ teaspoon freshly ground black pepper
¼ teaspoon stevia

4 ounces crumbled blue cheese

4 tablespoons Garlic Aioli (page 229)

2 tablespoons Dijon mustard

4 slices cooked bacon, halved

TO MAKE THE BUN

1. In a bowl, combine the potato noodles, scallions, almond meal, cheese, eggs, garlic powder, mustard, salt, and pepper. Mix well.

2. In a nonstick skillet, heat the olive oil over medium heat until it shimmers. Form the potato mixture into four patties and put them in the hot oil.

3. As they cook, press the fritters down with the spatula to flatten them.

4. Cook for about 5 minutes per side, until they are cooked through.

5. Allow the fritters to cool slightly.

TO MAKE THE CARAMELIZED ONIONS

1. In a large nonstick skillet, heat the olive oil over medium heat until it shimmers.

2. Add the onion, salt, and thyme.

3. Cook, stirring occasionally, until the onion is brown and caramelized, about 20 minutes.

CONTINUED

Bacon Cheeseburger
on a Potato Fritter Bun,
continued

TO MAKE THE BURGERS

1. Preheat the oven to 400°F.

2. Place a baking rack over a cookie sheet.

3. In a large bowl, combine the ground beef, fish sauce, garlic, salt, pepper, and stevia. Mix until well blended.

4. Form into four patties and put on the prepared baking sheet.

5. Bake until the ground beef registers an internal temperature of 145°F, about 20 minutes.

6. Turn off the oven, but leave the burgers in it. Sprinkle the blue cheese crumbles over each of the burgers. Close the oven and allow the cheese to melt, 3 or 4 more minutes.

TO ASSEMBLE

1. In a small bowl, mix together the aioli and the mustard. Spread each bun with the mixture.

2. Put one of the patties on top of the bun and top it with the bacon and caramelized onions.

Substitution tip: *For a sweeter bun, replace the potatoes with sweet potatoes or carrots.*

CARROT MAC AND CHEESE

PREP TIME: 10 MINUTES / COOK TIME: 10 MINUTES

HAND-CRANK
- Chipper blade
- Blade B

HOURGLASS
- Thick-cutting blade

SERVES 4

GLUTEN-FREE, VEGETARIAN

PER SERVING: Calories: 621;
Total Fat: 58g; Saturated Fat: 33g;
Cholesterol: 158mg;
Total Carbs: 12g; Fiber: 2g;
Protein: 16g

This stove-top version of mac and cheese has all the cheesy goodness of the original with just a fraction of the carbohydrates. It's also quick and easy to make. While this recipe uses carrot fettuccine, feel free to use your favorite spiralizable vegetable, such as a sweet potato or butternut squash.

6 carrots, peeled, ends cut flat,
    and spiralized into fettuccine noodles
2 tablespoons olive oil
¼ cup butter
½ cup heavy cream
8 ounces cream cheese, cubed
3 ounces mild Cheddar cheese, grated
3 ounces sharp Cheddar cheese, grated
½ teaspoon sea salt
¼ teaspoon freshly ground black pepper

1. Cut the carrots into individual elbow shapes.

2. In a large sauté pan, heat the olive oil over medium-high heat until it shimmers.

3. Add the carrot elbow noodles and cook, stirring occasionally, until al dente, about 5 minutes.

4. In a saucepan, heat the butter, heavy cream, and cream cheese over medium heat, stirring constantly, until the butter and cream cheese are melted.

5. Stir in the Cheddar cheeses. Cook, stirring constantly, until the cheese melts and the sauce is smooth.

6. Stir in the salt, pepper, and carrot elbow noodles. Stir to combine well and cook to warm the noodles through.

DAIKON RADISH SHRIMP FRIED RICE

PREP TIME: 15 MINUTES / COOK TIME: 15 MINUTES

HAND-CRANK
- Shredder blade
- Blade D

HOURGLASS
- Thin-cutting blade

SERVES 2

GLUTEN-FREE,
PALEO-FRIENDLY

PER SERVING: Calories: 449;
Total Fat: 34g; Saturated Fat: 5g;
Cholesterol: 452mg;
Total Carbs: 14g; Fiber: 3g;
Protein: 29g

Get your Chinese food fix with this delicious shrimp fried rice. The rice is made from daikon radish, which gives the rice a nice peppery bite. The great thing about fried rice is just how customizable it really is. You can make it vegan, Paleo-friendly, and everything in between by just switching a few ingredients.

1 daikon radish, peeled, ends cut flat,
    and spiralized into spaghetti noodles
4 tablespoons olive oil
6 scallions (white and green parts), sliced
1 carrot, peeled and minced
1 teaspoon grated ginger
8 ounces baby shrimp, cooked
3 garlic cloves, minced
2 eggs, beaten
2 tablespoons wheat-free tamari
    or coconut aminos

1. In a blender or food processor, pulse the daikon radish noodles until it resembles rice, 10 to 20 one-second pulses. Set aside.

2. In a large skillet, heat the olive oil over medium-high heat until it shimmers.

3. Add the scallions, carrot, and ginger and cook until the vegetables are soft, about 5 minutes.

4. Add the shrimp and cook, stirring occasionally, until warmed through, about 2 minutes.

5. Add the garlic and cook, stirring constantly, until it is fragrant, 30 to 60 seconds.

6. Add the eggs and cook, stirring constantly, until the eggs are scrambled and done, about 2 minutes.

7. Add the daikon radish rice and cook, stirring frequently, until the rice is tender, about 5 minutes.

8. Stir in the tamari.

Substitution tip: *Replace the shrimp with 4 ounces of cubed tofu and eliminate the egg to make this dish vegan.*

TATER TOT CASSEROLE

PREP TIME: 3 HOURS SOAKING PLUS 15 MINUTES ACTIVE PREP / COOK TIME: 1 HOUR

IDEAL FOR HAND-CRANK
SPIRALIZERS

- Shredder blade
- Blade D

SERVES 4

GLUTEN-FREE

PER SERVING: Calories: 614;
Total Fat: 28g; Saturated Fat: 12g;
Cholesterol: 144mg;
Total Carbs: 35g; Fiber: 8g;
Protein: 49g

Remember tater tot casserole from when you were a kid? The spiralized version turns it into more of a hash brown casserole. Still, the same flavors and crispy-creamy textures are there.

2 cups Basic Meat or Poultry Stock (page 225),
    made with beef

3 ounces dried porcini mushrooms

1 potato, peeled, ends cut flat, and spiralized
    into spaghetti noodles

1 tablespoon melted butter

1 teaspoon sea salt, divided

1 pound ground beef

2 tablespoons olive oil

1 onion, chopped

8 ounces crimini mushrooms, quartered

3 garlic cloves, minced

¼ cup arrowroot powder

1 teaspoon dried thyme

¼ teaspoon freshly ground black pepper

1 teaspoon dried mustard

2 tablespoons Worcestershire sauce

½ cup heavy cream

2 ounces Cheddar cheese, grated

1. In a small bowl combine the beef stock and dried porcini mushrooms. Let the mushrooms soak for 3 hours until soft.

2. Remove the mushrooms from the broth, squeeze out the liquid, and chop them. Set both aside.

3. Preheat the oven to 400°F.

4. In a large bowl, toss the potato noodles with the melted butter and ½ teaspoon of the salt. Set aside.

5. In a large skillet over medium-high heat, cook the ground beef, crumbling with the side of a spoon. Cook until browned, about 5 minutes. Remove the ground beef from any fat in the pan with a slotted spoon and set it aside.

6. Add the olive oil to the pan and heat until it shimmers. Then add the onion, reserved porcini mushrooms, crimini mushrooms, and garlic, and cook, stirring occasionally, until they are soft, about 5 minutes.

7. Whisk the arrowroot powder into the reserved broth. Add it to the pan with the vegetables along with the thyme, the remaining ½ teaspoon of salt, the pepper, mustard, and Worcestershire sauce.

8. Cook, stirring frequently, until the mixture thickens, about 5 minutes. Stir in the heavy cream and the reserved ground beef. Cook, stirring constantly until it heats through, about 4 minutes.

9. Pour the mixture into a large bowl and stir in the cheese.

10. Pour the meat and cheese mixture into a 9-by-9-inch baking pan. Top it with the buttered potato noodles.

11. Bake in the preheated oven for 15 minutes. Reduce the heat to 350°F and continue baking until the potatoes are golden, about 40 minutes.

GROUND PORK CHOW MEIN

PREP TIME: 15 MINUTES / COOK TIME: 15 MINUTES

HAND-CRANK
- Shredder blade
- Blade D

HOURGLASS
- Thin-cutting blade

SERVES 4

GLUTEN-FREE,
PALEO-FRIENDLY

PER SERVING: Calories: 350;
Total Fat: 5g; Saturated Fat: 2g;
Cholesterol: 83mg;
Total Carbs: 42g; Fiber: 4g;
Protein: 35g

This stir-fried Chinese dish is utterly craveable. Unfortunately, classic versions contain gluten and lots of carbs. This pared-down version uses carrot noodles, which lower the carbs and add a tasty bite and slight sweetness.

1 pound ground pork
6 scallions (white and green parts), sliced
1 tablespoon grated ginger
1 (8-ounce) can sliced water chestnuts, drained
6 ounces shiitake mushrooms, sliced
6 carrots, peeled, ends cut flat, and spiralized
    into spaghetti noodles
3 garlic cloves, minced
½ cup Basic Meat or Poultry Stock (page 225),
    made with chicken
2 tablespoons arrowroot powder
2 tablespoons wheat-free tamari
    or coconut aminos
½ teaspoon homemade Sriracha (page 228)
    or store-bought

1. In a large skillet, cook the ground pork, crumbling with the side of the spoon, until it is browned, about 5 minutes.

2. Remove the pork from the fat with a slotted spoon and set it aside.

3. Using the pork fat in the pan, cook the scallions, ginger, water chestnuts, and shiitake mushrooms until soft, about 5 minutes.

4. Add the carrot noodles and cook, stirring occasionally, until they are al dente, about 5 minutes more.

5. Add the garlic and cook, stirring constantly, until it is fragrant, 30 to 60 seconds.

6. Return the ground pork to the pan.

7. In a small bowl, whisk together the chicken broth, arrowroot powder, tamari, and sriracha.

8. Stir the sauce into the carrot noodles. Cook, stirring constantly, until the sauce thickens slightly, about 3 minutes.

10

BAKED SWEETS

ZUCCHINI BREAD

PREP TIME: 15 MINUTES / COOK TIME: 45 MINUTES

HAND-CRANK

- Shredder blade
- Blade D

HOURGLASS

- Thin-cutting blade

MAKES 1 LOAF (12 SLICES)

GLUTEN-FREE,
PALEO-FRIENDLY,
VEGETARIAN

PER SLICE: Calories: 69;
Total Fat: 4g; Saturated Fat: 3g;
Cholesterol: 27mg; Total Carbs: 7g;
Fiber: 3g; Protein: 2g

Zucchini bread is pretty standard fare in the late summer and early autumn when all of the gardeners are overrun with zucchini and trying to share it with others. If you're so lucky as to have someone offer you their fresh, homegrown zucchini, snap it up. You can make this tasty bread.

2 tablespoons coconut oil, melted, divided
1 zucchini, ends cut flat and spiralized
    into spaghetti noodles
½ cup coconut flour
¾ teaspoon baking powder
½ teaspoon ground nutmeg
1 tablespoon ground cinnamon
¼ teaspoon stevia
¼ teaspoon salt
2 eggs
¼ cup coconut milk
1 very ripe banana, mashed

1. Preheat the oven to 350°F.

2. Grease a loaf pan with 1 tablespoon of coconut oil.

3. Cut the zucchini noodles into 1- to 2-inch pieces

4. In a large bowl, sift together the coconut flour, baking powder, nutmeg, cinnamon, stevia, and salt.

5. In a small bowl, whisk together the eggs, coconut milk, remaining 1 tablespoon of coconut oil, and mashed banana until well combined.

6. Add the wet ingredients to the dry ingredients and stir until just combined.

7. Fold in the zucchini noodles.

8. Pour the mixture into the prepared loaf pan and bake in the preheated oven until a toothpick inserted in the center comes out clean, about 45 minutes.

9. Cool on a wire rack.

Cooking tip: *Coconut flour is a very thirsty dry ingredient. Therefore, you want to work quickly after incorporating the wet ingredients with the dry so it doesn't soak up too much liquid.*

CARROT MUFFINS

PREP TIME: 15 MINUTES / COOK TIME: 25 MINUTES

HAND-CRANK
- Shredder blade
- Blade D

HOURGLASS
- Thin-cutting blade

MAKES 12 MUFFINS

GLUTEN-FREE,
PALEO-FRIENDLY,
VEGETARIAN

PER MUFFIN: Calories: 158;
Total Fat: 12g; Saturated Fat: 6g;
Cholesterol: 55mg; Total Carbs: 9g;
Fiber: 3g; Protein: 4g

Mashed bananas make this batter really moist and flavorful. These muffins make a terrific sweet treat or work really well for breakfast or a quick snack. The carrots add an earthy sweetness to these tasty muffins, and as long as you eat only one, your carb counts stay low.

3 carrots, peeled, ends cut flat,
    and spiralized into spaghetti noodles
1¼ cup almond meal
½ teaspoon baking powder
½ teaspoon baking soda
¼ teaspoon salt
¼ teaspoon stevia
1 tablespoon ground cinnamon
1 teaspoon ground ginger
2 very ripe bananas, mashed
4 eggs, beaten
¼ cup melted coconut oil
¼ cup coconut milk
1 teaspoon vanilla extract

1. Preheat the oven to 350°F.

2. Line 12 muffin cups with paper liners.

3. Cut the carrot noodles into 1 to 2-inch pieces and set aside.

4. In a large bowl, sift together the almond meal, baking powder, baking soda, salt, stevia, cinnamon, and ginger.

5. In a medium bowl, whisk together the mashed bananas, eggs, coconut oil, coconut milk, and vanilla extract.

6. Mix the wet ingredients into the dry ingredients, stirring until just combined.

7. Fold in the reserved carrot noodles.

8. Pour the batter into the prepared muffin cups.

9. Bake in the preheated oven until a toothpick inserted in the center comes out clean, about 25 minutes.

10. Cool on a wire rack before serving.

CHOCOLATE–BEET MUFFINS

PREP TIME: 15 MINUTES / COOK TIME: 25 MINUTES

 IDEAL FOR HAND-CRANK
SPIRALIZERS

- Angel hair blade
- Blade D

MAKES 1 DOZEN MUFFINS

GLUTEN-FREE,
PALEO-FRIENDLY,
VEGETARIAN

PER TABLESPOON: Calories: 174;
Total Fat: 14g; Saturated Fat: 3g;
Cholesterol: 27mg; Total Carbs: 8g;
Fiber: 2g; Protein: 6g

Spiralizer alternative: *If your
spiralizer doesn't make angel
hair, then use a box grater to
grate the beets instead.*

Beets have a natural sweetness that helps make these muffins taste like dessert, minus the usual added sugars. The earthy flavors of the beets blend beautifully with the chocolate in the muffins, as well. Almond butter keeps it all moist and imparts extra flavor.

3 beets, peeled, ends cut flat, and spiralized
    into angel hair noodles
2 tablespoons coconut flour
¼ teaspoon stevia
½ teaspoon baking soda
2 tablespoons unsweetened cocoa powder
¼ teaspoon salt
¼ cup coconut milk
1 cup almond butter, melted
1 teaspoon apple cider vinegar
2 eggs, beaten
1 teaspoon vanilla extract

1. Preheat the oven to 375°F.

2. Line 12 muffin cups with paper liners.

3. Cut the beet noodles into ½-inch pieces

4. In a large bowl, sift together the coconut flour, stevia, baking soda, cocoa powder, and salt.

5. In a medium-sized bowl, whisk together the coconut milk, almond butter, apple cider vinegar, eggs, and vanilla extract.

6. Mix the wet ingredients into the dry ingredients, taking care to not overmix.

7. Fold in the beets.

8. Pour the batter into the prepared muffin tins. Bake in the preheated oven until a toothpick inserted in the center comes out clean, about 25 minutes. Cool on a wire rack before serving.

AVOCADO–CHOCOLATE MOUSSE
ON SPICED SWEET POTATO NESTS

PREP TIME: 15 MINUTES / COOK TIME: 20 MINUTES

 IDEAL FOR HAND-CRANK
SPIRALIZERS

- Shredder blade
- Blade D

SERVES 4

GLUTEN-FREE,
PALEO-FRIENDLY, VEGAN

PER CUP: Calories: 432; Total
Fat: 41g; Saturated Fat: 16g;
Cholesterol: 0mg; Total Carbs: 22g;
Fiber: 14g; Protein: 5g

Spiralizer alternative: *If you
have an hourglass spiralizer,
you can substitute 6 large carrots for the sweet potatoes.*

*Bake these sweet and crispy sweet potato nests in the oven, and
then serve them with a scoop of this tasty chocolate mousse.
The mousse is dairy-free, so it's perfect for Paleo and vegan
diets. It's also really delicious; something chocolate lovers will
completely appreciate.*

FOR THE SWEET POTATO NESTS

2 sweet potatoes, peeled, ends cut flat,
    and spiralized into spaghetti noodles
2 tablespoons coconut oil, melted
¼ teaspoon stevia
1 teaspoon ground cinnamon
½ teaspoon ground ginger
Pinch of salt

FOR THE MOUSSE

3 avocados, peeled and pitted
¼ cup coconut milk
½ teaspoon ground cinnamon
½ cup unsweetened cocoa powder
1 teaspoon stevia
1 teaspoon vanilla extract
Pinch of salt
1 teaspoon orange zest

1. Preheat the oven to 450°F.

2. Place the oven rack in the top third of the oven.

3. In a large bowl, toss together the sweet potato noodles, coconut oil, stevia, cinnamon, ginger, and salt.

4. Form the potatoes into four nests and arrange them on a nonstick baking sheet.

5. Bake in the preheated oven until the nests are crisp, 15 to 20 minutes.

6. Cool on a wire rack.

TO MAKE THE MOUSSE

1. In the bowl of a food processor, combine all of the mousse ingredients.

2. Process until smooth, 30 to 60 seconds.

3. Spoon the mousse onto the cooled sweet potato nests to serve.

PEAR CRISP

PREP TIME: 20 MINUTES / COOK TIME: 45 MINUTES

IDEAL FOR HAND-CRANK
SPIRALIZERS

- Chipper blade
- Blade B

SERVES 4

GLUTEN-FREE,
PALEO-FRIENDLY, VEGAN

PER SERVING: Calories: 439;
Total Fat: 32g; Saturated Fat: 14g;
Cholesterol: 0mg; Total Carbs: 37g;
Fiber: 10g; Protein: 8g

Spiralizer alternative: *Although the hourglass-shaped spiralizers can make the thick shape sought in this recipe, they're not ideal for use with pears. Instead, you can use a vegetable peeler, or even a sharp knife, to slice the pears.*

In autumn, when the days start to get a little bit of crispness in the air, pears are in season. Nothing suits the season better than a delicious fruit crisp, made with pears and a sweet, crumbly topping. You can also make this crisp with spiralized apples.

4 pears, stemmed, ends cut flat,
  and spiralized into fettuccine noodles
½ teaspoon lemon zest,
  plus 1 teaspoon lemon juice
½ teaspoon stevia
½ teaspoon sea salt, divided
2 teaspoons ground cinnamon, divided
½ teaspoon ground ginger
¾ cup chopped walnuts
¼ cup coconut flakes
¼ cup almond meal
¼ cup coconut oil, melted

1. Preheat the oven to 350°F.

2. Cut the pear noodles into 2-inch pieces.

3. In a large bowl, mix together the pear noodles, lemon zest and juice, stevia, ¼ teaspoon of the salt, 1 teaspoon of the cinnamon, and the ginger.

4. Pour the mixture into a 9-by-9-inch baking pan.

5. In a medium bowl, combine the walnuts, coconut flakes, almond meal, remaining ¼ teaspoon of salt, remaining 1 teaspoon of cinnamon, and coconut oil. Mix well.

6. Sprinkle the mixture on top of the pear noodles.

7. Bake the pear crisp in the preheated oven until the topping is browned and the pear noodles are tender, 40 to 45 minutes.

Substitution tip: *You can replace the chopped walnuts with chopped pecans, if you wish. The pecans are a little bit sweeter naturally.*

LEMON CUSTARD
WITH PEAR TOPPING

PREP TIME: 15 MINUTES / COOK TIME: 90 MINUTES, PLUS 1 HOUR COOLING

IDEAL FOR HAND-CRANK
SPIRALIZERS

- Shredder blade
- Blade D

SERVES 6

GLUTEN-FREE,
PALEO-FRIENDLY,
VEGETARIAN

PER SERVING: Calories: 352;
Total Fat: 31g; Saturated Fat: 26g;
Cholesterol: 82mg;
Total Carbs: 18g; Fiber 5g;
Protein: 6g

Spiralizer alternative: *If you
don't have the ability to make
the wide noodles on your
spiralizer, you can also use a
vegetable peeler to make them.*

*Lemon-flavored custard is sweet and refreshing without being
overwhelming in flavor. The mild, juicy, spiced pear noodles on
top add a lovely fresh contrast to the creamy coconut milk custard. Cook the custard in a water bath to keep it from scalding
or curdling.*

FOR THE CUSTARD

3 eggs, beaten
½ teaspoon stevia
3 cups coconut milk
1 teaspoon vanilla extract
1 tablespoon lemon zest

FOR THE PEARS

2 pears, stemmed, ends cut flat, and spiralized
    into spaghetti noodles
¼ teaspoon stevia
1 teaspoon ground cinnamon
½ teaspoon ground anise

TO MAKE THE CUSTARD

1. Preheat the oven to 300°F.

2. Fill a 9-by-13-inch baking pan half full with boiling
water and put it in the oven.

3. In a large bowl, combine the eggs, stevia, coconut milk,
vanilla extract, and lemon zest. Whisk until they are
well combined.

4. Pour the custard into six ramekins and put the ramekins
in the hot water bath in the oven.

5. Bake until the middle of the custards no longer jiggle but the outsides do, about 75 to 90 minutes.

6. Cool the custard on a wire rack for 1 hour, and then transfer them to the refrigerator.

TO MAKE THE PEARS

1. In a large bowl, combine the pear noodles, stevia, cinnamon, and anise.

2. Serve the pear noodles on top of the custard.

Substitution tip: *You can use orange zest or lime zest in place of the lemon for a different flavored custard.*

BUTTERNUT SQUASH MUFFINS

PREP TIME: 20 MINUTES / COOK TIME: 25 MINUTES

IDEAL FOR HAND-CRANK
SPIRALIZERS

- Angel hair blade
- Blade D

MAKES 12 MUFFINS

GLUTEN-FREE,
PALEO-FRIENDLY, VEGAN

PER MUFFIN: Calories: 98;
Total Fat: 7g; Saturated Fat: 6g;
Cholesterol: 0mg; Total Carbs: 9g;
Fiber: 3g; Protein: 2g

Spiralizer alternative: *If you
have an hourglass spiralizer,
you can substitute 2 large
carrots and cut the noodles
into 1-inch pieces or use a box
grater to grate the butternut
squash instead.*

*Butternut squash is wonderfully sweet, which adds sweetness
to these sugar-free muffins. The muffins don't contain eggs, so
they are slightly denser than muffins that do contain them,
but they are delicious.*

½ medium butternut squash, peeled, ends cut
  flat, spiralized into angel hair noodles
½ cup coconut flour
Zest of 1 orange
1 teaspoon ground cinnamon
¼ teaspoon ground cloves
2 very ripe bananas, mashed
¼ cup coconut oil, melted
1 teaspoon vanilla extract
¼ cup coconut milk

1. Preheat the oven to 350°F.

2. Line 12 muffin cups with paper liners.

3. Cut the butternut squash noodles into 1-inch pieces.

4. In a large bowl, whisk together the coconut flour, orange
zest, cinnamon, and cloves.

5. In a medium bowl, whisk together the bananas, coconut
oil, vanilla extract, and coconut milk.

6. Pour the wet ingredients into the dry ingredients and stir
until just combined.

7. Fold in the butternut squash noodles.

8. Pour the batter into the prepared muffin tins. Bake in
the preheated oven until a toothpick inserted in the center
comes out clean, 20 to 25 minutes.

9. Cool on a wire rack.

APPLE KUGEL

PREP TIME: 15 MINUTES / COOK TIME: 60 MINUTES

IDEAL FOR HAND-CRANK SPIRALIZERS

- Straight blade
- Blade A

SERVES 8

GLUTEN-FREE,
PALEO-FRIENDLY,
VEGETARIAN

PER SERVING: Calories: 350;
Total Fat: 25g; Saturated Fat: 16g;
Cholesterol: 61mg;
Total Carbs: 30g; Fiber 4g;
Protein: 5g

Spiralizer alternative: *If you
don't have the ability to make
the wide noodles on your
spiralizer, you can also use a
vegetable peeler to make them.*

*Traditionally, baked apple kugel is made from egg noodles.
Here, the apples become the noodles thanks to the spiralizer.
The dish is traditionally served on Jewish holidays.*

4 apples, stemmed, cored, ends cut flat,
   and spiralized into ribboned noodles

3 eggs

½ cup plus 3 tablespoons coconut oil,
   melted, divided

½ teaspoon stevia

½ cup freshly squeezed orange juice

1 cup almond meal flour, divided

¼ cup tapioca flour

1½ teaspoons ground cinnamon, divided

¼ teaspoon salt

1 teaspoon vanilla extract

1. Preheat your oven to 350°F.

2. Grease a 9-by-13-inch baking pan with 1 tablespoon
of coconut oil.

3. Cut the apple noodles into 2-inch pieces.

4. In a large bowl, beat the eggs. Beat in ½ cup coconut oil,
stevia, orange juice, ¾ cup almond meal, tapioca flour,
1 teaspoon cinnamon, salt, and vanilla extract.

5. Fold in the apple noodles.

6. In a small bowl, mix the remaining ¼ cup almond meal
with the remaining ½ teaspoon cinnamon and 2 tablespoons
remaining melted coconut oil. Sprinkle the mixture over the
top of the kugel.

7. Bake in the preheated oven until a toothpick inserted in
the center comes out clean, about 1 hour.

11

KITCHEN STAPLES

BASIC VEGETABLE STOCK

PREP TIME: 10 MINUTES / COOK TIME: 10 TO 24 HOURS

Making vegetable stock in your slow cooker is super easy and hands off. Save all of your vegetable trimmings in a zipper bag in the freezer and dump them in the slow cooker with water. You can save trimmings from carrots, mushrooms, celery, zucchini, fennel, onions, and leeks. Avoid strongly flavored trimmings such as broccoli, cabbage, and radish.

2 onions, roughly chopped
4 carrots, roughly chopped
6 celery stalks, roughly chopped
1 fennel bulb, roughly chopped
4 ounces mushrooms
6 garlic cloves, smashed
2 rosemary sprigs
2 thyme sprigs
½ cup fresh parsley
16 peppercorns
1 teaspoon sea salt
1 bay leaf
8 cups water

1. In a 6-quart slow cooker, combine all of the ingredients. Cover and simmer for 10 to 24 hours.

2. After the stock has cooled slightly, strain through a fine mesh colander. Discard the solids.

3. Stock will keep for up to 6 months in the freezer.

Cooking tip: *Freeze the stock in 1-cup servings so you always have some.*

BASIC MEAT OR POULTRY STOCK

PREP TIME: 10 MINUTES / COOK TIME: 12 TO 24 HOURS

MAKES 8 CUPS

GLUTEN-FREE,
PALEO-FRIENDLY

PER CUP: Calories: 38;
Total Fat: 1g; Saturated Fat: 0g;
Cholesterol: 0mg; Total Carbs: 1g;
Fiber 0g; Protein: 5g

Once again, the slow cooker is a champ at making stock, because it is so hands off. You can make this stock on the stovetop. Just simmer it, uncovered, for 3 to 4 hours. The stock freezes for up to 6 months or refrigerates for up to 1 week. You can use vegetable trimmings to flavor this stock, as well.

2 to 4 pounds beef, pork, or poultry bones
1 onion, roughly chopped
2 carrots, roughly chopped
2 celery stalks, roughly chopped
16 peppercorns
6 garlic cloves, smashed
1 teaspoon sea salt
2 rosemary sprigs
2 thyme sprigs
8 cups water, or enough to cover the bones

1. In a 6-quart slow cooker, combine all of the ingredients. Cover and cook on low for 12 to 24 hours.

2. Strain through a fine mesh sieve and discard the solids.

3. Refrigerate overnight, covered. Skim the hardened fat from the top and discard it.

Cooking tip: *To smash garlic, lay it on a cutting board and press the flat side of a knife over it. Strike the knife (avoiding the blade) sharply with the heel of your hand.*

BASIL VINAIGRETTE

PREP TIME: 5 MINUTES

MAKES: 1 CUP

GLUTEN-FREE,
PALEO-FRIENDLY, VEGAN

PER 2 TABLESPOONS:
Calories: 166; Total Fat: 19g;
Saturated Fat: 3g;
Cholesterol: 0mg; Total Carbs: 1g;
Fiber 0g; Protein: 0g

The great thing with vinaigrette is that you can use it in a variety of ways. It makes a delicious salad dressing, as well as a tasty marinade for meat, poultry, or fish. Vinaigrette is made with a standard ratio of three parts oil to one part acid, such as vinegar or citrus juice. The Dijon mustard acts as an emulsifier to hold the oil and vinegar together. From there, you can add all sorts of flavorings.

¾ cup extra virgin olive oil

¼ cup red wine vinegar

1 teaspoon Dijon mustard

1 tablespoon finely minced shallot

1 garlic clove, finely minced

¼ cup chopped fresh basil

½ teaspoon sea salt

¼ teaspoon freshly cracked pepper

Whisk all of the ingredients together in a small bowl until well combined.

Substitution tip: *Replace the red wine vinegar with lemon and replace the basil with oregano for a Mediterranean-inspired dressing.*

RANCH DRESSING

PREP TIME: 5 MINUTES

MAKES: 2½ CUPS

GLUTEN-FREE, VEGETARIAN

PER 2 TABLESPOONS:
Calories: 71; Total Fat: 6g;
Saturated Fat: 3g;
Cholesterol: 11mg; Total Carbs: 3g;
Fiber 0g; Protein: 1g

Whether you love or want to love salads, this recipe for a not-quite-classic ranch will make sure you get your recommended dose of veggies in. By preparing the dressing at home you can be sure there are no added sugars or thickeners in it that are counterproductive to your health goals. The ingredient list may look a tad long, but it's worth buying the fresh herbs to pack this go-to dressing full of flavor.

1 cup sour cream
½ cup mayonnaise
½ cup heavy whipping cream
2 tablespoons almond milk
2 teaspoons freshly squeezed lemon juice
1 teaspoon apple cider vinegar
¼ cup chopped fresh parsley
2 tablespoons chopped fresh dill
1 tablespoon chopped fresh chives
1 garlic clove, minced
½ teaspoon salt
½ teaspoon freshly ground black pepper
⅛ teaspoon cayenne pepper
Dash of Tabasco sauce

In a small bowl, whisk together all of the ingredients until well blended.

SRIRACHA

PREP TIME: 10 MINUTES / COOK TIME: 10 MINUTES

MAKES 1 CUP

GLUTEN-FREE,
PALEO-FRIENDLY, VEGAN

PER TABLESPOON: Calories: 25;
Total Fat: 0g; Saturated Fat: 0g;
Cholesterol: 0mg; Total Carbs: 5g;
Fiber 1g; Protein: 1g

Sure, you can buy sriracha at the grocery store, but why not make your own? That way, you can precisely control what is in it. Sriracha adds wonderful heat to foods, and it has become a very popular condiment. This recipe uses healthy, delicious ingredients.

1½ pounds spicy red chile peppers, such as red
    jalapeño (hotter peppers make hotter sriracha)
½ cup apple cider vinegar
10 garlic cloves, finely minced
¼ cup tomato paste
1 tablespoon whole-wheat tamari
    or coconut aminos
½ teaspoon stevia
1 teaspoon sea salt

1. Stem, seed, and chop the chile peppers.

2. In a food processor or blender, combine all of the ingredients and purée until smooth.

3. In a small saucepan, bring the purée to a simmer over medium-high heat and cook, stirring frequently, for about 10 minutes, until it is thick.

4. Store in a sterile container in the refrigerator for up to 1 month.

Cooking tip: *Wear gloves when working with the peppers.*

GARLIC AIOLI

PREP TIME: 10 MINUTES

Aioli is basically flavored mayonnaise. While you could just mix herbs and spices into mayonnaise you buy at the store, that stuff is loaded with chemicals and sweeteners like high-fructose corn syrup. This aioli, on the other hand, uses only wholesome ingredients like eggs, oil, vinegar, and spices.

2 garlic cloves, minced
2 egg yolks
2 tablespoons red wine vinegar
¼ teaspoon sea salt
½ teaspoon Dijon mustard
1½ cups extra virgin olive oil

1. In the bowl of a food processor, combine the garlic, egg yolks, vinegar, salt, and mustard.

2. Turn on the food processor and process. Working through the spout, add the oil, a drop at a time until about 20 drops are incorporated. Then add the oil in a thin stream until the mayonnaise emulsifies.

3. The aioli will keep in the refrigerator for up to 1 week.

Cooking tip: *If you don't have a food processor, you can still make mayonnaise—it just takes a little elbow grease. Whisk the minced garlic, egg yolks, vinegar, salt, and mustard in a bowl, and add the olive oil while whisking constantly, first in drips, and then in a thin stream. Eventually, if you continue to whisk it will emulsify into mayonnaise.*

KETCHUP

PREP TIME: 10 MINUTES / COOK TIME: 10 MINUTES

MAKES ¾ CUP

GLUTEN-FREE,
PALEO FRIENDLY, VEGAN

PER TABLESPOON: Calories: 16;
Total Fat: 0g; Saturated Fat: 0g;
Cholesterol: 0mg; Total Carbs: 3g;
Fiber 1g; Protein: 1g

Ketchup is another condiment that's loaded with chemicals, sugar, and high-fructose corn syrup. Not only is the stuff you can make at home better for you, but it's a lot more flavorful, as well. Once you have the basic recipe down, you can adjust the herbs and spices to suit your own tastes.

6 ounces tomato paste
¼ cup water
2 tablespoons apple cider vinegar
2 garlic cloves, minced
1 teaspoon ground cinnamon
¼ teaspoon ground nutmeg
1 teaspoon onion powder
¼ teaspoon stevia
Pinch cloves
¼ teaspoon orange zest
1 teaspoon gelatin powder

1. In a saucepan, combine all of the ingredients. Bring them to a simmer and cook until it reaches your desired consistency. If it is too thick, add a little more water.

2. This ketchup will store in a tightly sealed container for up to 4 weeks.

NUT BUTTER SAUCE

PREP TIME: 10 MINUTES

MAKES 1½ CUPS

GLUTEN-FREE,
PALEO-FRIENDLY, VEGAN

PER 2 TABLESPOONS:
Calories: 168; Total Fat: 15g;
Saturated Fat: 9g;
Cholesterol: 0mg; Total Carbs: 7g;
Fiber 2g; Protein: 5g

Nut butter sauce, such as peanut or almond sauce, is great on noodles, with vegetables, or as a sauce for meats. This nut butter sauce has a nice Asian flair. If you are Paleo, you'll want to avoid peanut and cashew sauce and stick with almond sauce.

¼ cup nut butter, such as peanut, cashew,
   or almond
8 ounces coconut milk
½ cup lime juice
½ teaspoon stevia
½ cup whole-wheat tamari or coconut aminos
1 garlic clove, minced
½ teaspoon grated ginger
1 teaspoon homemade Sriracha (page 228)

Whisk together all the ingredients until well combined.
Store for up to 4 weeks in a tightly sealed container.

THE DIRTY DOZEN
& THE CLEAN FIFTEEN

A nonprofit and environmental watchdog organization called the Environmental Working Group (EWG) looks at data supplied by the US Department of Agriculture (USDA) and the Food and Drug Administration (FDA) about pesticide residues. Each year it compiles a list of the lowest and highest pesticide loads found in commercial crops. You can use these lists to decide which fruits and vegetables to buy organic to minimize your exposure to pesticides and which produce is considered safe enough to buy conventionally. This does not mean they are pesticide-free, though, so wash these fruits and vegetables thoroughly.

These lists change every year, so make sure you look up the most recent one before you fill your shopping cart. You'll find the most recent lists as well as a guide to pesticides in produce at EWG.org/FoodNews.

2015 Dirty Dozen

Apples	Peaches	*In addition to the dirty dozen, the EWG added two produce contaminated with highly toxic organo-phosphate insecticides:*
Celery	Potatoes	
Cherry tomatoes	Snap peas (imported)	
Cucumbers	Spinach	
Grapes	Strawberries	Kale/Collard greens
Nectarines (imported)	Sweet bell peppers	Hot peppers

2015 Clean Fifteen

Asparagus	Eggplants	Papayas
Avocados	Grapefruits	Pineapples
Cabbage	Kiwis	Sweet corn
Cantaloupes (domestic)	Mangoes	Sweet peas (frozen)
Cauliflower	Onions	Sweet potatoes

MEASUREMENT CONVERSION CHARTS

Volume Equivalents (Liquid)

US STANDARD	US STANDARD (OUNCES)	METRIC (APPROXIMATE)
2 tablespoons	1 fl. oz.	30 mL
¼ cup	2 fl. oz.	60 mL
½ cup	4 fl. oz.	120 mL
1 cup	8 fl. oz.	240 mL
1½ cups	12 fl. oz.	355 mL
2 cups or 1 pint	16 fl. oz.	475 mL
4 cups or 1 quart	32 fl. oz.	1 L
1 gallon	128 fl. oz.	4 L

Oven Temperatures

FAHRENHEIT (F)	CELSIUS (C) (APPROXIMATE)
250°	120°
300°	150°
325°	165°
350°	180°
375°	190°
400°	200°
425°	220°
450°	230°

Volume Equivalents (Dry)

US STANDARD	METRIC (APPROXIMATE)
⅛ teaspoon	0.5 mL
¼ teaspoon	1 mL
½ teaspoon	2 mL
¾ teaspoon	4 mL
1 teaspoon	5 mL
1 tablespoon	15 mL
¼ cup	59 mL
⅓ cup	79 mL
½ cup	118 mL
⅔ cup	156 mL
¾ cup	177 mL
1 cup	235 mL
2 cups or 1 pint	475 mL
3 cups	700 mL
4 cups or 1 quart	1 L

Weight Equivalents

US STANDARD	METRIC (APPROXIMATE)
½ ounce	15 g
1 ounce	30 g
2 ounces	60 g
4 ounces	115 g
8 ounces	225 g
12 ounces	340 g
16 ounces or 1 pound	455 g

REFERENCES

EWG. "EWG's Shopper's Guide to Pesticides in Produce." Summary. Accessed March 12, 2015. http://www.ewg.org/foodnews/dirty_dozen_list.php.

Maffuci, Ali. Inspiralized. Accessed March 12, 2015. http://www.inspiralized.com/.

National Foundation for Celiac Disease Awareness. "Celiac Disease: Fast Facts." Accessed March 12, 2015. http://www.celiaccentral.org/celiac-disease/facts-and-figures/.

National Foundation for Celiac Disease Awareness. "What Is Non-Celiac Gluten Sensitivity?" Accessed March 12, 2015. http://www.celiaccentral.org/non-celiac-gluten-sensitivity/introduction-and-definitions/.

"The New Way to Make a Homemade (Healthy!) Pasta Dinner." *Good Housekeeping.* (Accessed Sep. 30, 2014). http://www.goodhousekeeping.com/product-reviews/test-kitchen-blog/spiralizer-spiraled-vegetables.

Santos, F. L., S. S. Esteves, A. da Costa Pereira, W. S. Yancy Jr., and J. P. L. Nunes. "Systematic Review and Meta-Analysis of Clinical Trials of the Effects of Low Carbohydrate Diets on Cardiovascular Risk Factors." *Obesity Reviews* (July 2012), doi/10.1111/j.1467-789X.2012.01021.x/

"Spiral Slicers (Spiralizers)." *Cook's Illustrated.* Accessed March 12, 2015. http://www.cooksillustrated.com/equipment_reviews/1540-spiral-slicers-spiralizers.

WebMD. "Celiac Disease Treatment." Accessed March 12, 2015. http://www.webmd.com/digestive-disorders/celiac-disease/celiac-disease-treatment

RECILE INDEX

INDEX

C

CPSIA information can be obtained at www.ICGtesting.com
Printed in the USA
BVOW07s0922270815

415135BV00014B/57/P

9 781623 156022